lonely planet

LONELY PLANET
ROAD TRIP

CALIFORNIA
HIGHWAY 1

Paige R Penland

Lonely Planet Publications
Melbourne • Oakland • London • Paris

Road Trip California Highway 1
1st edition – October 2003

**Published by Lonely Planet
Publications Pty Ltd**
ABN 36 005 607 983
90 Maribyrnong St, Footscray, Victoria
3011, Australia

Lonely Planet Offices
Australia Locked Bag 1, Footscray,
Victoria 3011
USA 150 Linden St, Oakland, CA 94607
UK 72-82 Rosebery Ave, Clerkenwell,
London EC1R-4RW
France 1 rue du Dahomey, 75011 Paris

Photographs
The cover image is available for licensing
from Lonely Planet Images.
e lpi@lonelyplanet.com.au
W www.lonelyplanetimages.com

Cover photograph by
Michael Aw

ISBN 1 74059 582 3

text & maps © Lonely Planet Publications
Pty Ltd 2003
photos © photographers as indicated
2003

Printed through The Bookmaker
International Ltd
Printed in China

Contents

Introduction

Highway 1 is one of America's classic drives, arranged here from north to south. You'll see three very different Californias along the way: the sparsely populated North, with severely cut coastlines and towering redwoods; the dramatic Central Coast, with wondrous Big Sur as its centerpiece; and sunny Southern California, with wide, sandy beaches and sprawling metropolises.

Completed in 1937 after 18 years of construction, California's first Scenic Highway certainly deserves the title. Taking in the brilliant scenery here is mandatory: Immense, golden cliffs plummet down to the rock-strewn sea, which can change from peacock blue to the deep purple of a marlin's back in a heartbeat.

If you enjoy driving, you'll love the banks and swerves of this road. But your patience may be tested. Summer (in the north, especially) brings fog and heavy traffic, which can be deadly. Only two lanes wind around the deeply crevassed shoreline, so traffic can snarl behind a single RV for miles. Use the pullouts if there are more than five cars behind you – it's the law.

In winter, wind and waves conspire to tear down beaches, homes and chunks of freeway; even if the road is open to traffic, you may be driving at a crawl. The benefits of off-season travel, however, include migrating gray whales – the ultimate roadside attraction – while several coastal parks are home to wintering monarch butterflies.

Bring a swimsuit, a spare tire, camping gear and a sturdy pair of hiking shoes, plus a flattering outfit for exploring the cities along the way. Carry your camera at all times. Allow at least four days – or better, two weeks. And relax: The point of this trip, more than most, isn't the destination. Strict schedules and plans will only take away from the experience. Beauty has no address.

Getting There & Around

The two major airports nearest to Hwy 1 are the **San Francisco International Airport** (SFO; ☎ 650-876-7809; [w] www.flysfo.com) and **Los Angeles International Airport** (LAX; ☎ 310-646-5252; [w] www.lawa.org). While international travelers are stuck using these behemoths, domestic travelers can look into a number of smaller airports, also concentrated in the San Francisco and Los Angeles areas.

Dozens of rental car companies are stationed at airports large and small, and most require a credit card and proof that you're over 25 years old. The major nationwide rental car companies include Alamo (☎ 800-327-9633), Avis (☎ 800-321-3712), Budget (☎ 800-527-0700), Dollar (☎ 800-800-4000), Hertz (☎ 800-654-3131), National (☎ 800-328-4567) and Thrifty (☎ 800-367-2277). The California Driver Handbook, which is free at any DMV or at [w] www.dmv.ca.gov, explains California's road rules comprehensively.

Note that this isn't the easiest trip on your car, particularly north of San Francisco. If you're driving an older model, consider purchasing 24-hour roadside assistance from AAA (American Automobile Association; ☎ 800-874-7532; [w] www.aaa.com) in addition to your regular coverage.

Hwy 1 is a designated bicycle route, but rarely is there a designated strip of concrete for two wheelers along the narrow, winding roads. Keep your eyes open. And that goes for you bicyclists, too.

Itineraries

THE CLASSIC: ONE TO TWO WEEKS

Lucky you – you've got time to do Hwy 1 right.

From San Francisco, take Hwy 1 North to Leggett (a good four hours, at least), but spend the night in Laytonville or, better, Garberville. If you've got time, explore the Lost Coast or redwood forests that evening, then wake up early for the obligatory cruise through the Chandelier Drive-Thru Tree before hitting the dramatic Northern California coastline.

From Los Angeles, take I-5 down to Dana Point, a quick shot except during rush hour(s). The best places to stay at the bottom (unless you want to take in an Anaheim amusement park or two) are Laguna or Newport Beaches, perfect for unwinding before the overwhelming experience of LA's overpopulated urban environment. Then, it's north into the wilderness.

THE GREAT ESCAPE: THREE TO FOUR DAYS

Sure, you could do the whole road, but you'd miss the whole point. Instead, take a stretch slowly – it's about the journey, not the destination. Following are some options for a shorter trip, and all are just as lovely in reverse.

San Francisco to Leggett (3 days). Hike Point Reyes, brunch in Bodega Bay, collapse at a Mendocino B&B – it's a wilderness wonderland with epicurean tastes.

San Francisco to San Luis Obispo (3–4 days). From roller coasters and world-class aquariums to stunning Big Sur and outrageous Hearst Castle, this is the pride of Hwy 1.

San Francisco to Los Angeles or vice versa (at least 4 days). See the best of both Californias, from sandy southern beaches to the rocky northern coast. Some rental car companies let you pick up at one end and drop off at the other for a little extra cash.

Los Angeles to San Luis Obispo (2–3 days). Bring your board (or at least your swimsuit) for touring these world-class beaches. Allow an extra day to see the Channel Islands.

Los Angeles to Monterey (3–4 days). From palm trees to pine trees, red-tiled Santa Barbara to misty Monterey, you'll finally understand why everyone loves California.

THE GETAWAY: ONE TO TWO DAYS

Just pick a direction and go! It's that easy.

From San Francisco, you'll reach nature the fastest heading north, though the southern route offers more unusual 'urban' adventures. Escape from LA heading north into the megacity's stunning playgrounds, unless Laguna's art scene tempts you southward.

Highlights

Mendocino (p9): A bohemian resort town in a windswept coastal paradise

Point Reyes (p16): Wilderness long isolated by nature and humankind, wonderful for hiking

Golden Gate Bridge (p22): Walk n' roll across this engineering marvel and cultural icon

Santa Cruz (p26): Festive boardwalk roller coasters and Año Nuevo's amorous elephant seals

Big Sur (p35): Sublime coastlines + meditative hot springs = transcendence galore

San Luis Obispo (p40): Underrated and uncrowded, with chewing gum to spare

Venice Beach (p48): Humanity's insanities on colorful display

Laguna Beach (p57): Fine beaches and fine art make for one fine finale

From the Top: Leggett

POPULATION 200; MAP 1

An inauspicious start to California's prettiest ribbon of concrete, Leggett was described by local teens as 'a great place if you're a stoner or retiree.' Dining and lodging options are limited; better bets are Garberville (north on Hwy 101), Laytonville (south on Hwy 101) or Fort Bragg (see p8). The northern terminus of Hwy 1 is certainly beautiful, however, and has several gems to recommend it.

SIGHTS & ACTIVITIES

CHANDELIER DRIVE-THRU TREE

Begin your drive down Hwy 1 through this hollowed-out, 315-foot-tall redwood tree – it's a politically incorrect tradition. The surrounding park has 200 acres of virgin redwood forest with picnic areas and nature walks.

☎ 707-925-6363; $3 per vehicle; open 8am-dusk

CONFUSION HILL

It's either an excellent late-1940s tourist trap or an inexplicable warping of the Earth's gravitational forces. Not only can you walk the walls of a rustic cabin, there's also a half-hour train trip through the trees (adult/child $3/2; summer only) and what may be the largest redwood sculpture in the world.

☎ 707-925-6477; 75001 N Hwy 101; adult/child $3/2; open 8am-7pm

SLEEPING & EATING

STANDISH-HICKEY STATE RECREATION AREA
Shady campsites overlook South Fork Eel River, where you can swim in summer and fish for steelhead trout in winter. There are a few short hiking trails to keep the kids busy, too.

☎ 707-925-6482, reservations ☎ 800-444-7275; W www.reserveamerica .com; 69350 Hwy 101; campsites $11-14; day-use $2 per vehicle

REDWOODS RIVER RESORT
North of Leggett and across Hwy 101 from Confusion Hill, this family-oriented private campground has redwoods and short hiking trails.

☎ 707-925-6249; W www.redwoodriverresort.com; 75000 Hwy 1; rooms $69-115, cabins $74-99, rustic cabins $35, tent/RV sites $18/30

GARSKE'S LEGGETT MARKET & DELI
The closest thing to a grocery store in this neck of the woods, Garske's has dry goods, deli sandwiches and a small produce section.

☎ 707-925-6000; Hwy 271; sandwiches $4-6; open 8am-9pm

NE-BOB'S
Although there are several diners on Drive-Thru Tree Rd, Ne-Bob's, with a pleasant patio and decent home-style dishes, is your best bet.

☎ 707-925-1066; 62674 Drive-Thru Tree Rd; meals $4-11

BEST BOOKSTORES
Need some beach reading? Pop into one of these independent bookstores:

Gallery Bookshop ☎ 707-937-2665; 319 Kasten St, Mendocino
Point Reyes Books ☎ 415-663-1542; 11315 State Route 1, Point Reyes Station
Depot Book Store ☎ 415-383-7012; 87 Throckmorton Ave, Mill Valley
GGNPA/Muir Woods Muir Woods
Bookshop Santa Cruz ☎ 831-460-3254; 1520 Pacific Ave, Santa Cruz
Capitola Book Cafe ☎ 831-462-4415; 1475 41st Ave, Capitola
Bookworks Aptos ☎ 831-688-4554; 36 Rancho Del Mar Ctr, Aptos
Bay Books ☎ 831-375-0277; 316 Alvarado St, Monterey
Thunderbird Bookshop ☎ 831-624-1803; 3600 The Barnyard, Carmel
Phoenix Books ☎ 805-543-3591; 990 Monterey St, San Luis Obispo
Chaucer's Bookstore ☎ 805-682-4067; Loreto Plaza, 3321 State St, Santa Barbara
Pacific Travelers Supply ☎ 805-963-4438; 12 W Anapamu, Santa Barbara
Small World Books ☎ 310-399-2360;1407 Ocean Front Walk, Venice
Warwick's Books ☎ 858-454-0348; 7812 Girard Ave, La Jolla

On the Road

With Leggett behind you, you'll descend 800 feet within 20 winding miles, a narrow knot you'll share with logging trucks, RVs and high-powered (but poorly driven) sports cars.

You may glimpse water through the very tall trees, but nothing can prepare you for your first good look at the finest coastline this side of Norway. You want dramatic? You've got it.

Crumbling gray cliffs to the north explain why Hwy 1's coastal cruise must end: No road could long withstand nature's wildness around here. Which is precisely why the scene is so stunning.

You can actually continue north along the coastal Usal Rd (CR 431; impassable when wet) to **Sinkyone Wilderness State Park** (☎ 707-986-7711; tent sites $3-11), a 7300-acre preserve with 10 primitive camp-grounds scattered along the 22-mile **Lost Coast Trail**.

To the south, **Westport-Union Landing State Beach** (☎ 707-937-5804; campsites $7, day-use $1) is the first really tempting stretch of sand along the highway. If it's full, continue on to **Wages Creek Beach Campground** (☎ 707-964-2964; 37700 Shoreline Hwy; campsites $18, day-use $5), with hot showers and other creature comforts.

The pastel collection of Cape Cod Victorians called **Westport** has lots of B&Bs: Try antique-packed **Lost Coast Inn** (☎ 707-964-5584; 38921 N Hwy 1; rooms $70-90), which also operates the local bar. Bring dinner, however. Tiny **Westport Community Store** (☎ 707-964-2872; 37701 N Hwy 1; open 7am-9pm), with snacks and a deli, is the only restaurant.

MacKerricher State Park (☎ 707-937-5804, reservations ☎ 800-444-7275; W www.reserveamerica.com; campsites $12) offers seal viewing,

---

DETOUR: NORTH THROUGH THE BIG TREES

More accommodating than Leggett, **Garberville** (population 2000) has budget hotels and good camping at Richardson Grove State Park (☎ 707-247-3380; tent/RV sites $12-18, day-use $2).

The Garberville detour passes several fine redwood attractions, including the cozy One Log House (☎ 707-247-3717; 705 Hwy 1; admission $1; open 8am-7:30pm), a hollowed-out tree that's bigger than some San Francisco apartments. Just north is Grandfather Tree Gifts (☎ 707-247-3413; open 9am-6pm), where you can purchase a redwood of your very own.

Can't stop? Continue north to **Phillipsville**, where you'll exit Hwy 101 to the Avenue of the Giants, through Humboldt Redwoods State Park and more drive-through trees. The gift shops here are great: Hobbiton, USA (☎ 707-923-2265; 1111 Ave of the Giants; open 10am-7pm), for example, features cast-concrete characters from the Tolkien trilogy.

If you're still unsatisfied, pick up a copy of Lonely Planet's *California* guide and continue north to visit awe-inspiring **Redwood National Park**.

tidepooling and almost 20 miles of hiking and biking trails. Across Hwy 1, **Ricochet Ridge Ranch** (☎ 707-964-7669; ☒ www.horse-vacation.com; 24201 N Hwy 1; rides start at $80) lets you explore it on horseback.

Locals love **Purple Rose Restaurant** (☎ 707-964-6507; 24300 N Hwy 1; dinner $6-11; open 5-9pm Wed-Sun), with great Mexican food and better margaritas.

Fort Bragg

POPULATION 6500; MAP 1

It's the closest thing to a thriving metropolis in the region, with super-markets, drug stores, ethnic restaurants and relatively inexpensive lodging. Unlike many towns along California's north coast, Fort Bragg doesn't rely on tourism – thus, it's more functional than quaint. But if you're willing to ignore the occasional traffic light and the rows of log-ging trucks waiting behind it, you'll find plenty to entertain you.

SIGHTS & ACTIVITIES

SKUNK TRAIN
Take a half-day ride through the redwoods on one of three antique trains, including a modified steam engine known as 'Old 45.' For a bit extra, you can overnight in Willits, a shady inland town well worth an evening's exploration.

☎ 707-964-6371, 800-777-5865; ☒ www.skunktrain.com; E Commercial St; adult/child $35/17 (under 5 free)

GLASS BEACH
Just north of Fort Bragg, this former dump is named for the sea-polished glass lying on the sands. It's reached by a short headlands trail leading toward the sea from Elm St.

WHALE WATCHING
From December through March, you can spot gray whales making their way between Mexico and Alaska. **Anchor Charters** (☎ 707-964-4550) offers two-hour excursions for $70 per person, as well as rock cod– and salmon-fishing trips.

WHERE THE REDWOODS ARE

There are two California redwoods: The giant Sequoia, available only in the Sierra Nevada (150 miles due east), and the coastal red-wood, in no shortage around Leggett.

Coastal redwoods are special not only for their size (many top 300 feet) and age (2000 years, easy), but also for their primitive method of reproduction. The tiny seeds are rarely fertile, so red-woods rely on *burls* (lumps of reproductive tissue) along the base of the trunk to clone themselves; root systems remain intimately attached. These woods are more like a mushroom fairy ring than a regular pine forest.

Dozens of roadside shops hawk burls and young trees; only skilled gardeners should even bother with the delicate burls. A sapling at least 3 feet tall is far more likely to survive. Keep in mind that the redwood's range is limited to foggy coastal areas as far south as Big Sur.

HEADLANDS COFFEEHOUSE

Not a typical coffee shop, this art gallery and performance space hosts live entertainment nightly. Check their website or just stop by to see what's on.

☎ 707-964-1987; W www.headlandscoffeehouse.com; 120 Laurel St; open 7am-10pm Sun-Thu, 7am-11pm Fri-Sat

SLEEPING & EATING

Dozens of inexpensive, charmless hotels make a great budget alternative to Mendocino's pretty but pricey B&Bs.

WOODSIDE RV PARK & CAMPGROUND

Just a mile out of town, this private campsite is popular with RVers but has a nicely wooded section for tents as well.

☎ 707-964-3684; campsites $16-28

COLOMBI MOTEL

A bit off the strip and a better deal because of it, you'll get clean rooms for a fair price, once you find the office (across the street at the grocery store).

☎ 707-964-5773; 647 Oak St; rooms $55-60

EGGHEADS RESTAURANT

Breakfast is served all day (plus burgers and sandwiches after 11am), including more than 50 omelets, some made with locally caught Dungeness crab.

☎ 707-964-5005; 326 N Main St; entrees $3-9; open 7am-2pm

NORTH COAST BREWING COMPANY

It's got good, hearty California cuisine and even better organic beer – try the Old Rasputin Imperial Russian Stout. The convivial atmosphere is an added bonus.

☎ 707-964-2739; 444 N Main St; lunch $5-10, dinner $9-22; open 11:30am-10pm

On the Road

The shoreline here is downright breathtaking; stop and inhale deeply at **Mendocino Botanical Gardens** (☎ 707-964-4352; 18220 N Hwy 1; adult/child $6/3; open 9am-5pm), with 47 perfumed acres of roses, camellias and more.

If you'd rather walk on the wild side, continue to **Jug Handle State Reserve**, where the famed 5-mile **Ecological Staircase** hike takes you through five glaciated terraces with distinct (and weird) ecosystems, including a rare and fragile pygmy forest.

Caspar is known best for the **Caspar Inn** (☎ 707-964-5565; W www.casparinn.com; rooms with shared bath $65), a nice enough inn with one of the area's top music venues. Dance 'til the wee hours to some eclectic live music (the schedule is online) and crawl upstairs to bed after the show.

If there's no room at the inn, try **Caspar State Beach** (☎ 707-937-3306; Point Cabrillo Dr; campsites $18), popular with hardy surfers and kayakers.

Mendocino

POPULATION 1200; MAP 1

Beautiful and bohemian Mendocino, once an all-but-abandoned lumber settlement, is now a top destination for power-relaxers fleeing San Francisco in search of spiritual refreshment.

The entire town, packed with lovingly restored Cape Cod–style and Victorian homes, is on the National Register of Historic Places. The setting is stunning; the air actually sets the US standard for freshness. Cute shops, quaint B&Bs, rejuvenating spas and great restaurants complete the picture. Stay a while.

SIGHTS & ACTIVITIES

Locals will tell you that the Mendo experience is about relaxing, indulging and not seeing or doing much. Still, there are some sights that are well worth seeing.

POINT CABRILLO LIGHTHOUSE
This 1909 lighthouse has been restored and is open to the public, the center-piece of a 300-acre preserve crisscrossed with trails. Guided walks on ecology and history start at 11am Sunday (May-Sep).

☎ 707-937-0816; Point Cabrillo Dr; free; open 9am-5pm

MENDOCINO ART CENTER
This community gem puts on exhibitions, arts and crafts fairs, plus surprisingly high-quality live theater year-round.

☎ 707-937-5818, 800-653-3328; w www.mendocinoartcenter.org; 45200 Little Lake St; gallery open 10am-5pm

GALLERY WALKS
Grab a free *Gallery Map* anywhere in town, or (better) join the **art walk** on the second Saturday evening of each month (Apr-Dec; 6-9pm), when artists break out the wine and cheese.

MUSEUMS
If the weather's brisk, stop into the **Ford House** (☎ *707-937-5397; 735 Main St; admission $1 donation; open 11am-4pm)*, which doubles as a park headquarters and information center, or **Kelley House Museum** (☎ *707-937-5791; 45007 Albion St; admission $2; open 1-4pm)* in a restored 1861 home. Both are labors of love featuring inventive natural and local history displays.

SWEETWATER SPA
Enjoy shared or private hot tubs and saunas, which you can top off with a mas-sage or even stretch into an overnight at their excellent inn (pets welcome).

☎ 707-937-4140; w www.sweetwaterspa.com; 955 Ukiah St; tub and/or sauna $9-16/hr; open noon-10pm; Sweetwater Inn rooms $110-295.

CATCH A CANOE & BICYCLES TOO!
California's newest state park, **Big River Reserve**, has the longest undeveloped estuary in Northern California; explore it on a bike ($10/30 hr/day), single kayak ($12/36), double kayak ($18/64) or canoe ($8-22/hr).

☎ 707-937-0273, 800-320-2453; open 9am-5:30pm

HIKING
This region has outstanding hiking. **Mendocino Headlands State Park**, which surrounds the town, has several short, kid-friendly hikes overlooking bluffs and rocky coves. Heartier souls should try the rambling, 7-mile **Falls Loop Trail**, in Russian Gulch State Park (see Sleeping), complete with a 36-foot waterfall. Maps of many more area trails are available at the Ford House (see Museums).

SLEEPING

Mendocino Vacations (☎ *707-937-5033; w www.mendocinovacations .com)* can help with last-minute B&B and vacation rentals.

MENDOCINO CAMPGROUND
Uphill from Hwy 1, this shady campsite is convenient to town and has hot showers.

☎ 707-937-3130; Comptche-Ukiah Rd; campsites $19; open Apr-Oct

RUSSIAN GULCH STATE PARK

Two miles north of town, this popular park is famous for Devil's Punch Bowl, a collapsed sea cave where waves slosh noisily, as well as excellent hiking.

☎ 800-444-7275; W www.reserveamerica.com; campsites $12

BLACKBERRY INN

North of town, rooms at this quirky but comfy Old West–themed motel are about as budget as it gets around here.

☎ 707-937-5281, 800-950-7806; 44951 Larkin Rd; rooms $95-145

MENDOCINO HOTEL

This luxuriously restored 1878 Victorian hostelry overlooks the sea. The hotel restaurant serves up premium dishes at prices to match.

☎ 707-937-0511, 800-548-0513; W www.mendocinohotel.com; 45080 Main St; rooms with/without baths from $120/95, suites $275

JOSHUA GRINDLE INN

The Inn pampers its guests with gourmet breakfasts, free cookies and local wines; the watertower rooms are claustrophobic but comfortable.

☎ 707-937-4143, 800-474-6353; W www.joshgrin.com; 44800 Little Lake Rd; rooms $130-245

EATING

TOTE FÊTE BAKERY

For the sort of picnic upon which Bently owners slather Grey Poupon, grab your gourmet sandwiches, sweets and salads right here.

☎ 707-937-3383; 10450 Lansing St; deli food $3-8; open 10:30am-7pm Mon-Sat, 10:30am-4pm Sun

LIPINSKI'S MENDO JUICE JOINT

This funky, laid-back local fave juices just about anything that grows, and serves up espresso and pastries to counter any health gains you might have just made.

☎ 707-937-1111; 10483 Lansing St; treats $3-6

MENDO BURGERS

At this old-fashioned lunch counter tucked away at the rear of Mendocino Bakery & Cafe, having it your way can include veggie, chicken, turkey and fish burgers.

☎ 707-937-1111; 10483 Lansing St; burgers $3-5; open 11am-5pm

THE RAVENS

Most of the big B&Bs and hotels have fine restaurants charging $15 to $30 for dinner. The Ravens stands out with an entirely vegetarian menu, much of it grown in the gardens around the attached **Stanford Inn** (W www.stanfordinn .com; rooms $245-720).

☎ 707-937-5615; W www.ravensrestaurant.com; Comptche-Ukiah Rd; entrees $11-30; open 7:30-11am & 5:30-8:30pm

CAFE BEAUJOLAIS

Better known as the 'Beauj,' this is *the* spot, with elegant dining in a cozy 1893 Victorian farmhouse, complete with excellent service and organic offerings. Jeans and/or ball gowns are acceptable.

☎ 707-937-5614; 961 Ukiah St; California cuisine $18-25; open 5:45-9pm

On the Road

One mile south of town, **Van Damme State Park** (☎ 707-937-4016, reservations ☎ 800-444-7275; W www.reserveamerica.com; campsites $12, day-use $5) has sea caves for kayaking and 2- to 8-mile **Fern Canyon**

Trail looping through the pygmy forest, where century-old pines are about a foot tall.

From here, Hwy 1 wends inland, which means that *both* sides of the road are thick with B&Bs. **Albion River Campground** (☎ 707-937-0606; *tent/RV sites $19/27*) is popular among fishers, and the onsite **Flats Café** *(fast seafood $3-8; open 6am-2pm Apr-Nov)* serves a mean clam chowder.

Elk (population 200) is a collection of cute Victorians overlooking the spectacular rocky outcroppings thrusting upward just offshore. Of the town's many B&Bs (W www.elkcoast.com has complete listings), **Harbor House Inn** (☎ 707-877-3203; 5600 S Hwy 1; rooms $300-400, breakfast $12, dinner $45) is the plushest of them all. Your splurge includes a gourmet breakfast and four-course prix-fixe dinner; non-guests can also partake (reservations required).

For a tipple try **Bridget Dolan's Irish Pub** (☎ 707-877-3422; 5910 S Hwy 1; pub grub $7-15; open 5-9pm), with wine and (lots of) beer. Or head up the long driveway to **Beacon Light Cocktails by the Sea** (7401 S Hwy 1; open 5-11pm Fri-Sat), with 13 bar stools, no fancy beer and no live music, but Elk's only liquor license. Tips support the volunteer fire department.

You'll notice that the windswept seaside has suddenly sprouted a suburban subdivision. This is **Irish Beach** (☎ 707-882-2467, 800-882-8007; W www.irishbeach.com; vacation rentals $120-300), which rents furnished family homes sleeping six or more, complete with hot tubs.

The town of **Manchester** has a grocery store plus one world-renowned natural wonder: **Manchester State Beach** (☎ 707-937-5804; primitive campsites $5-7), where the San Andreas fault plunges into the sea. The 4-mile **Alder Creek Trail**, along the driftwood-littered coast, begins near the appealing campsites.

Point Arena Lighthouse (☎ 707-882-2777; W www.pointarenalight house.com; 45500 Lighthouse Rd; adult/child $4/1; open 11am-3:30pm) offers lighthouse tours with great views of the whale migrations, as well as a few plush rooms ($170-300).

Too pricey? Between the lighthouse and Hwy 1, **Rollerville Junction** (☎ 707-882-2440; 22900 Shoreline Hwy S; tent/RV sites $26/32, cabins with/ without water $95/48) is downscale and fun.

After all this unadulterated nature, **Point Arena** (population 600) seems downright urban. Everything's organic, from **El Burrito** (☎ 707-882-2910; 165 Main St (Hwy 1); Mexican-hippy fusion cuisine $3-8; open 11:30am-7pm), with great tofu rancheros, to **Pangaea Café** (☎ 707-882-3001; 250 Main St; California cuisine $19-25; open 6-10pm), known all over NorCal for top-notch fine dining.

The **Sea Shell Inn** (☎ 707-882-2000; 135 Main St; singles/doubles start at $50/70) is an excellent deal on a clean, comfortable room. For nightlife, see what's on at the **Point Arena Cinema** (☎ 707-882-3456; W www.arena cinema.com), where blockbusters and independent flicks alternate with live music. Or play some pool at the coffee shop across the street.

Point Arena's tiny tourist quarter, **Arena Cove**, overlooks a dramatic shoreline beloved by surfers, sea kayakers and deep-sea fishers. Inexpensive food and luxurious accommodations, including the restored 1901 **Coast Guard House B&B** (☎ 707-822-2442; W www .coastguardhouse.com; 695 Arena Cove; rooms $125-195) make this a pleasant detour.

Schooner Gulch Rd, off Hwy 1, accesses three public beaches, including **Bowling Ball Beach**, which at low tide displays a strange assortment of absolutely round boulders polished smooth by the waves.

Anchor Bay Campground (☎ 707-884-4222; w www.abcamp.com; 35400 S Hwy 1; campsites $27-38, day-use $2) is the perfect place to pitch a tent (or park your RV – permanently), with a great beach and shady path into the town of **Anchor Bay**. 'Town' has a couple of art galleries, a Mexican restaurant and **Wineworld** (☎ 707-884-4245; 35501 Shoreline Hwy; open 8am-8pm), an impressive organic grocer with some 150 different local and imported wines.

The big city here is **Gualala** (population 800), boasting supermarkets, restaurants and a dive shop, **Jay Baker True Value Hardware** (☎ 707-884-3534; 38820 S Hwy 1; open 8am-5pm), which also sells camping supplies.

It's a great place to sleep: **Gualala River Redwood Park** (☎ 707-884-3533; 46001 Hwy 1; tent/RV sites $34/40) is private and plush, while **Gualala Point Regional Park** (☎ 707-785-2377; campsites $16, day-use $3) has beach access and the lovely 2-mile **Headlands-Beach Loop Trail**.

The 1903 **Gualala Hotel** (☎ 707-884-3441; rooms with/without private bath $120/85), offers clean rooms, an ornate **restaurant** (dinner $18, other meals $5-9; open 9am-2pm daily, 5-10pm Fri-Sun) with live music on weekends, and **George**, the ghost of a former owner's son. He enjoys turning the water on and off.

Stretching southward for 10 developed miles is **Sea Ranch** (☎ 707-785-2371; w www.searanchlodge.com; 60 Sea Walk Dr; rooms $144-395, houses start at $300), a pricey vacation community with golf packages, fancy restaurants and a private airport. Six of its beaches are open to the public (parking $3), as is tranquil **Sea Ranch Chapel** (40033 Hwy 1; admission free), as spiritually satisfying as the rest of Sea Ranch is silly.

Lovelier **Salt Point State Park** (☎ 707-847-3221, reservations ☎ 800-444-7275; w www.reserveamerica.com; campsites $12-18) has miles of coastline, including **Stump Beach**, with spectacular driftwood displayed along a scenic 3-mile trail. There's also a pygmy forest and **Kruse Rhododendron State Reserve**, with lots of bright flowers in spring.

Less crowded **Stillwater Cove Regional Park** (☎ 707-847-3245; campsites $16, day-use $3) has perfect camping, a sandy cove and the rewarding 1-mile **Stockoff Creek Loop Trail**.

Fort Ross State Historic Park (☎ 707-847-3286; admission $2; open 10am-4pm) has several short hiking trails and a full-sized replica of the

FARMERS MARKETS

Like your food fresh from the field? Farmer's markets, which usually run May through October, are a North Coast tradition.

Fort Bragg: Wednesday 3:30-6pm; cnr Laurel & Franklin Sts
Mendocino: Friday noon-2pm; cnr Howard & Main Sts
Albion: Sunday 2-4pm; Albion Grocery (off Hwy 1)
Gualala: Saturday 3-5pm; Gualala Community Center (off Hwy 1)
Boonville: Saturday 9:45am-noon; Boonville Hotel

1812 Russian fort that once supplied Russia's Alaskan colonies. Just south of the park is **Fort Ross Reef** (☎ 707-847-3286; campsites $12), with picturesque and somewhat primitive sites.

Jenner (population 300) is the next major town, overlooking an extravagant sandbar formed by the embrace of the Russian River and Pacific Ocean. There's a gas station/deli and a few upscale restaurants and B&Bs poised precariously above the encroaching ocean.

Bodega Bay

POPULATION 900; MAP 1

Bodega Bay is an actual fishing village, an endangered species in California. Sure, there are B&Bs aplenty, and whale-watching season fills 'em up. But this isn't another Mendocino, as April's popular **Bodega Bay Fishermen's Festival** celebrates. The tiny town of Bodega, a few miles inland from Bodega Bay, was the setting for Alfred Hitchcock's film *The Birds*.

SIGHTS & ACTIVITIES

BODEGA HEAD
Jutting out into the ocean, this windswept park is a great place to whale watch in January and February, or see the seals rut in November. There's good hiking too – try the 2-mile **Bodega Head Loop** trail.

FISHING
If you prefer your fish as fresh as possible, charter a boat like **Wil's Fishing Adventure** (☎ 707-875-2323; 1580 Eastshore Rd; trips start at $30) for Dungeness crab, salmon or rock cod. Whale-watching trips are also available.

DETOUR: ANDERSON VALLEY & BOONVILLE

For a change of pace from ocean views, head 27 scenic, winding miles east on Mountain View Rd to **Anderson Valley**, home to dozens of unusual wineries (W www.avwines.com), and the small town of **Boonville**.

Boonville is famous for two things: Boontling, a 'language' developed a century ago by isolated locals (modern locals will make fun of you if you try to use it), and the Anderson Valley Brewing Company (☎ 707-895-2337; W www.avbc.com; 17700 Hwy 253; free tours at 1:30pm & 4pm), with eight award-winning beers you can sample onsite.

It's worth staying a while – try upscale Boonville Hotel & Restaurant (☎ 707-895-2210; 14050 Hwy 128; rooms $85-225, entrees $11-22), with small but airy gem-colored rooms.

Cheaper digs can be had at amazing Hendy Woods State Park (☎ 707-937-5804; campsites $12, rustic cabins $20), a virgin redwood forest with some wonderful short trails. Don't miss the Apple Farm (☎ 707-895-2461; 18501 Greenwood Rd), next door, with organic apple cider and the best apples I have ever eaten.

SURF SHACK

Enjoy paradise in a kayak ($45/85 4 hrs/day), on a bike ($5/hr) or on a surfboard ($25/day); surfing lessons run $109.

☎ 707-875-3944; W www.bodegabaysurf.com; 1400 Hwy 1

BODEGA BAY PRO DIVE

Get tips on the top spots, up-to-date information and diving equipment ($60/day for everything) at this excellent dive shop.

☎ 707-875-3054; 1275 Hwy 1

GOURMET AU BAY

With more than 90 local wines and dozens more exotic vintages, this cozy wine-tasting room lets you imbibe 11 different wines (or champagnes, on Sunday) on a deck overlooking the Bay. They call it 'wine surfing.'

☎ 707-875-9875; 913 Hwy 1; wine board $6; open 11am-6pm

SLEEPING & EATING

BODEGA DUNES

With trail access to Bodega Head, fabulous bluff-top sites and great fishing and tidepooling almost right from your tent, this is an excellent place to set up camp.

☎ 800-444-7275; W www.reserveamerica.com; campsites $12

DORAN REGIONAL PARK

The tidal estuary along this windswept jetty of sand, surf and scrub keeps the birds and birders migrating back year after year.

☎ 707-527-2041; campsites $16, day-use $3

INN AT THE TIDES

The parking lot can hold several tour buses, but rooms are semi-swanky and the **restaurant** (dinner $15-35; open 8am-9pm) has a great view. Try the Cajun snapper.

☎ 707-875-2751, 800-541-7788; W www.innatthetides.com; 800 Hwy 1; rooms $189-299

STARFISH

This upscale eatery emphasizes seafood and locally grown produce, but it's the view, overlooking spare rocks and crashing waves, that makes it special.

☎ 707-875-2513; 1400 Hwy 1; entrees $8-16; open 11am-9pm Mon-Fri, 8am-9pm Sat-Sun

On the Road

Continue south, winding inland through golden hills to tiny **Tomales**, with a small hotel, a couple of delis and the best grocery store around.

The Dillon Beach Rd turnoff heads west to downscale **Dillon Beach**, where you can pitch a tent in the dunes at **Lawson's Landing** (☎ 707-878-2443; tent/RV sites $5/15), where folks cure and can their catch right there. A shuttle (adult/child $3/1) runs at very low tides to an offshore sandbar, known for giant clams.

Hwy 1 soon intercepts the San Andreas Fault, filled with the deep Pacific and known as Tomales Bay – check it out in a kayak from **Támal Sáka** (☎ 415-663-1743; W www.tamalsaka.com; kayak $25/day, guided tour $60), in the small town of **Marshall** (population 500).

Barbecued oysters are the local specialty, and **Tony's Seafood Place** (☎ 415-663-1831; 18863 Hwy 1; entrees $5-16; open 11am-9pm Tue-Sun) does 'em right.

Point Reyes Peninsula

Map 1

Geologists believe this 110-square-mile triangle of land was torn by tectonics from the coastline 300 miles south, then dragged north over the millennia, en route to Seattle. For now it's home to **Point Reyes National Seashore** and **Tomales Bay State Park**, accessible from an assortment of adorable towns including Inverness, Olema and Point Reyes Station.

Most of the peninsula remains rugged wilderness; there are no drive-in campsites, but there are 150 miles of trails, encompassing mountains, tidepools, streams and forests.

SIGHTS & ACTIVITIES

HIKING

The **Bear Valley Visitor Center** (☎ 415-663-1200; W www.ptreyes.com; open 9am-5pm) has maps and up-to-date trail and camping information. Some of the finest trails include the wheelchair-accessible **Earthquake Trail** (1 mile), an interpretive loop exploring area geology; **Point Reyes Lighthouse** (1 mile), with one of the best whale-watching spots around; **Coast-Laguna Loop** (5 miles), with great views and easy access from the youth hostel; and **Tomales Point Trail** (7 miles), where you're likely to run into elk.

CYCLE ANALYSIS

As the pun indicates, a tour de Point Reyes will do more for your emotional well-being than almost any couch. Rent mountain bikes, tandems and accessories starting at $10/hour or $28/day for tackling the numerous bike trails.

☎ 415-663-9164; W www.cyclepointreyes.com; Hwy 1 in Olema; open 10am-4pm Fri-Sun Apr-Nov, or by appointment

FIVE BROOKS STABLE

Make reservations in advance for one- to six-hour ($30-150) horseback rides through the wilderness. Hayrides are just $5.

☎ 415-663-1570; W www.fivebrooks.com; 8001 Hwy 1; rides start at $30

ART STUDIOS

With all this beauty, it's unsurprising that Point Reyes Station, Inverness and Olema are packed with art galleries. Find information on openings through **Point Reyes Open Studios** (W www.pointreyesart.com).

SONOMA COUNTY'S BEST BEACHES

The Sonoma County Beaches stretch along 15 miles, with some 20 rugged (and dangerous – watch kids closely) beaches to choose from. Favorites include:

Goat Rock Beach: The rock, home to lots of harbor seals, is off-limits; the challenging 3-mile Kortum Trail is not.

Shell Beach: This is a must for geologists and other rock hounds.

Wright Beach (☎ 707-865-2391; campsites $12): Your tent never had such a stunning view.

Duncan's Landing: AKA 'Death Rock' – no swimming, OK?

Bodega Dunes (☎ 800-444-7275; W www.reserveamerica.com; campsites $12): Camp among the soft dunes.

SLEEPING

For information on dozens of area inns, contact **Point Reyes Lodging** (☎ 415-663-1872, 800-539-1872; W www.ptreyes.com).

HIKE-IN CAMPING
Point Reyes features four popular hike-in (or boat-in) campsites, all with untreated water and grills; make reservations. **Coast Camp** (2.8 miles from trailhead) is on the Coast Trail; **Sky Camp** (3 miles) is at 1,025 feet on Mt Wittenberg; **Glen Camp** (4.6 miles) requires traversing two canyons; and **Wildcat Camp** (5.6 miles), close to Alamere Falls, is the most popular.

☎ 415-663-8054, reservations accepted 9am-2pm Mon-Fri; campsites $10

OLEMA RANCH CAMPGROUND
It's not as pretty as the park's primitive campsites, but does have hot showers, pull-through RV sites and flush toilets.

☎ 415-663-8001, 800-655-2267; W www.olemaranch.com; Hwy 1; tent/RV sites $23/32

POINT REYES HOSTEL
At the heart of the peninsula, this fine hostel has no TV, no Internet access and, by the way, cell phones don't work out here. It does have kitchen facilities and one of the best backyards of any hostel ever.

☎ 415-663-8811; dorm beds $14/7 adult/child; lockout 10am-4:30pm

MANKA'S INVERNESS LODGE
This refurbished 1917 hunting lodge is heavy on old-world charm, from elegant rooms and comfy cabins to a Czech-inspired eatery emphasizing wild game.

☎ 415-669-1034; W www.mankas.com; Argyle St; rooms $185-425

EATING

TOMALES BAY FOODS
It's actually three separate (wonderful) markets: **Indian Peach Food Co**, with an excellent deli; **Cowgirl Creamery**, with local cheeses; and **Golden Point Produce**, where it's all organic. It's the perfect place to pack a picnic.

☎ 415-663-8478; 80 4th St, Point Reyes Station; open 10am-6pm Wed-Sun

PINE CONE DINER
It's got Formica counters and blue-plate specials, but organic and free-range options distinguish this local landmark. Servers recommend the gravlox omelet and corned-beef hash.

☎ 415-663-1536; 60 4th St, Point Reyes Station; diner food $6-16; open 8am-8:30pm Tue-Sun

VLADIMIR'S CZECHOSLOVAK RESTAURANT & BAR
Vladimir escaped communism (on skis!) and came to Inverness, where he's been dishing up meaty signature delicacies like lamb shank, wiener schnitzel, and goulash for more than 40 years.

☎ 415-669-1021; 12785 Drake Blvd, Inverness; lunch $9-14, dinner $11-36; open 11am-2pm & 5-10pm

Bolinas

POPULATION 1100; MAP 1

Just south of Point Reyes is one of Northern California's more mythic destinations, the hard-to-find hippy haven of Bolinas. Why is it so hard to find? Because locals remove the road signs. Sheesh.

Tip: Head west on the paved (but probably unmarked) Olem-Bolinas Rd, just a few hundred feet north of prominent Bolinas Lagoon. But remember that there's a reason why these folks have gone to all this trouble to keep you, the marauding tourist, away. Respect their insular customs and enjoy the sleepy pace. It's not exactly the friendliest place on Hwy 1, although some locals thankfully do go against the grain and smile welcomingly.

SIGHTS & ACTIVITIES

POINT REYES BIRD OBSERVATORY
Take winding Mesa Rd past the delicate Coast Guard communications array to the Bird Observatory, where you can watch biologists catch our feathered friends in 'mist nets,' then label, study and set them free. Hours are erratic; call ahead.

☎ 415-868-1221; W www.prbo.org; Mesa Rd

AGATE BEACH
Watch erosion in motion at this rapidly disintegrating beach, located at the bottom of the staircase, at the end of Elm St. Parking is tight, but tidepooling is sweet and it does have the single best park bench in the state.

BOBO BIKES
Rent wheels for $35 a day, then enjoy the area's awesome mountain biking trails – if you can get anyone to tell you where they are.

☎ 415-497-0688; 6 Wharf Rd; open Wed-Sun 10am-5pm

SLEEPING & EATING

SMILEY'S SCHOONER SALOON & HOTEL
If you're looking for a local bar, you've found it – bar stools, classic-rock cover bands on weekends and even some conversation, if you're lucky. Behind the saloon are pleasant cottages that almost qualify for B&B status – if that second 'B' stood for beer.

☎ 415-868-1311; 41 Wharf Rd; rooms $74-84

BLUE HERON INN
Rooms are intimate and homey; the upscale restaurant specializes in meatier elements of California cuisine. Breakfast is out of this world.

☎ 415-868-1102; W www.blueheron-bolinas.com; 11 Wharf Rd; rooms $125; dinner $13-22; restaurant open 5:30-9pm Thu-Mon

COAST CAFÉ
Almost everything is harvested within 25 miles of home – organic veggies, free-range salmon – and they make great wild-rice pancakes. Best of all, they seem somewhat tourist-friendly, a rare and wonderful thing.

☎ 415-868-2298; Wharf Rd; entrees $4-13

On the Road

South of Bolinas, Hwy 1 dips so low that it seems the lagoon might one day rise over the tarmac. Visit resident great blue herons and snowy egrets at **Audubon Canyon Ranch** (☎ 415-868-9244; w www.egret.org; 4900 Hwy 1; donations appreciated; open 10am-4pm Sat-Sun Mar-Jul), open only during the birds' dating and mating seasons.

Stinson Beach

POPULATION 751; MAP 2

Once just another peaceful collection of art galleries and veggie-friendly restaurants fronting a fine stretch of sand, this rapidly developing enclave is becoming a bedroom community for the cities due south. But it's still a quality beach town surrounded by some seriously stunning wilderness areas.

SIGHTS & ACTIVITIES

STINSON BEACH
It's got white sand, big waves, and beach bums and bunnies flirting all summer long – just like Southern California, but foggy and cold. Except on those sunny fall days…

☎ 415-868-0942; open 9am-10pm

RED ROCK BEACH
Marin County's most popular nude beach is about a mile south of Stinson Beach; note that the path down the bluffs is steep, so do wear shoes.

MUIR WOODS NATIONAL MONUMENT
Even when the paved walkways beneath these stately old-growth redwoods get horribly crowded, steep, 3-mile **Ocean View Trail** always seems to have breathing room. Or hike to **Muir Beach**, a picturesque cove (also accessible by car) with a nude strip just north.

☎ 415-388-2595; admission $2; open 8am-sunset

MOUNT TAMALPAIS STATE PARK
The 2571-foot peak of Mt Tam, as it's affectionately known, is criss-crossed by more than 50 miles of hiking trails and the first and most famous mountain bike runs in the world. The **East Peak Visitors Center** (☎ *415-388-2070; 801 Panoramic Hwy; open 7am-10pm*) has maps and information.

SLEEPING & EATING

STEEP RAVINE CAMPGROUND
Perched atop the buffs – er – bluffs, these sites overlook famed Red Rock Beach, accessible via the short, steep **Rocky Point Trail** right from camp. A few sites have very primitive cabins.

☎ 800-444-7275; W www.reserveamerica.com; campsites $15

STINSON BEACH MOTEL
Though not the first choice of honeymooning millionaires, rooms are clean and comfortable, plus it's right on the main drag.

☎ 415-868-1712; 3416 Hwy 1; rooms start at $65

PARKSIDE CAFE
It is not just a 'turkey club sandwich', it is an 'applewood smoked turkey on a seeded roll with roasted bell pepper aioli'. Ah, gentrification.

☎ 415-868-1272; 43 Arenal Ave; dinner $12-20, other meals $6-10; open 8am-4pm & 5-9:30pm

PELICAN INN
Right next to Muir Beach, this British-themed inn, bar and restaurant serves meaty, pricey meals, or you can munch cheaper grub in the pub while playing darts next to a roaring fire. Rooms are small but nice.

☎ 415-383-6000; 10 Pacific Way; entrees $10-22, rooms start at $200

On the Road

The highway south of Stinson Beach has been described as majestic, gorgeous, God's own road, and damned difficult without power steering. No matter; there are plenty of pullouts should you need to relax and enjoy the scenery while the sports cars vroom by.

Marin Headlands

MAP 2

These majestic golden hills (hence the name 'Golden Gate'; the bridge is actually international orange) rise from the water to enfold hiking and biking trails, historic military sites and a few very affluent communities. And the view – the mist-enshrouded liberal Avalon of San Francisco, a dozen perfect islands and a handful of delicate bridges – is one of the best things in life, and it's free.

SIGHTS & ACTIVITIES

Stop by the **Marin Headlands Visitors Center** (☎ 415-331-1540; Bunker Rd; open 9:30am-4:30pm) at Fort Barry for trail maps.

MARINE MAMMAL CENTER

Between the oil tankers, pleasure boats and pollution, sea mammals sometimes get into trouble; come see the recuperating cuties here, where scientists and volunteers nurse sick and hurt critters back to health.

☎ 415-289-7325; 1065 Fort Cronkhite; donations appreciated; open 10am-4pm

HEADLANDS CENTER FOR THE ARTS

They were once military barracks but are now studios, and several are open to the public. Consider taking some fine art home as part of your own personal peace dividend.

☎ 415-331-2787; W www.headlands.org; 944 Fort Barry; admission free; open 9am-5pm Mon-Fri, noon-5pm Sat-Sun

HIKING & BIKING

You could fill a book (there are several, actually) with area trails. Some top spots to stretch your legs include: 1-mile **Point Bonita Lighthouse** with a tunnel *and* suspension bridge; 2-mile **Tennessee Valley Trail**, near Mill Valley, mellow enough for the family; and the 2- to 6-mile **Coastal Trail**, which connects Forts Cronkhite and Barry with a steep, awesome trek popular among mountain bikers.

WHALE WATCHING

Gray whales migrate annually between the rich and frigid waters of Alaska to the balmy calving grounds of Baja every year. Removed from the Endangered Species List in 1995, almost 30,000 of the enormous critters make the 5000-mile journey, a commute that has whale-watchers waiting for winter.

The peak of the southern migration is January, but if you're hoping to see those precious newborns (weighing in at a mere 2000 pounds – awwww), check out the northerly March migration. New mothers often stay close to shore, where they can better defend against predators.

Point Reyes Lighthouse is just one spot where you can look for plumes, often the best way to find your first whale. But almost every point and peninsula along the West Coast provides a grand view of the beasts, or you can charter a boat for a closer look.

SLEEPING

Budget travelers can find clean, inexpensive rooms aplenty along Hwy 101, just north of the intersection with Hwy 1, where there is a strip of chains and family-owned hotels.

CHINA CAMP STATE PARK

Take the North San Pedro exit from Hwy 101 to this beautiful walk-in campground (sites are just a few hundred feet from the parking lot), with great hikes and smashing views.

☎ 415-456-0766, reservations ☎ 800-444-7275; **W** www.reserveamerica .com; campsites $1

HI MARIN HEADLANDS HOSTEL

It's a historic (1907) hostel in paradise, with narrow bunks, shared kitchen and one of the finest locations in the Bay Area.

☎ 415-331-2777; **W** headlandshostel.homestead.com; Bunker Rd; dorm beds $15, private rooms $45

On the Road

As you leave the Marin Headlands, you'll be dumped onto Hwy 101, which may be a bit of a shock: Five lanes of traffic, fifth gear and a $5 toll to cross the most famous bridge in the USA, the Golden Gate. But your first glimpse of San Francisco is breathtaking. In the distance, white buildings spill down 43 hills to the blue bay dotted with sailboats and islands. On a clear day, it's impossibly lovely; on a foggy day, however, it's impossible to see.

San Francisco

POPULATION 777,000; MAP 2

Capturing a city like San Francisco – which ranks as a world-class destination for reasons enough to fill a dozen books – in this amount of space is a job best left for haiku masters and Beat poets. Rather than trying to cover the city itself, this guide sticks to the coastline. If you'll be here any length of time, grab a copy of Lonely Planet's *San Francisco* or *Best of San Francisco* guides to squire around town. For restaurant, nightlife and event information, pick up one of the free weeklies available just about anywhere: the *San Francisco Bay Guardian* (**W** www.sfbg.com), and the *SF Weekly* (**W** www.sfweekly.com).

Hwy 1 does not take you through the city's most scenic areas. If you're just cruising by, take the following detour instead, so that you'll enjoy the Pacific rather than the concrete. Take the first exit on your right after you cross the Golden Gate Bridge. This leads onto Merchant Rd, a small road in the wooded heart of the **Presidio**. Follow Merchant to Lincoln Blvd, where you'll make a right. Lincoln winds through this former military base turned national park, then abruptly enters the upscale neighborhood of Sea Cliff. Marvel at the mansions (including the home of actor Robin Williams) with their enviable views. Follow the road as it runs into El Camino del Mar and enters **Lincoln Park**. The road curves past the **Palace of the Legion of Honor**, one of SF's best museums, then meanders through the **Lincoln Park Golf Course**, a public 18-hole course with spectacular views. Leaving Lincoln Park, make a right onto Clement St and drive toward the looming ocean. Round **Sutro Heights Park** to the Great Highway, along whose length stretches popular **Ocean Beach**. Coast along the Great Highway, which eventually merges with Hwy 1.

Better yet, get a room and spend a couple of days here; your wallet will suffer but your soul will thank you. Amazing ethnic neighborhoods, excellent architecture, multitudes of museums and some of the best shopping and bar-hopping on the planet are just a few of the draws.

SIGHTS & ACTIVITIES

GOLDEN GATE BRIDGE

It's big, it's orange and it's the pride of San Francisco. The classic photo is from well-signed **Vista Point**, north of the bridge; more artsy shots can be had at **Fort Point**, beneath the southern end, with a bonus Civil War–era fort and great fishing. (Movie buffs will also recognize this spot from *Vertigo*.) The walk across is a classic.

☎ 415-556-1693; W www.goldengate.org

THE PRESIDIO

Once a low-key and scenic army base, the Presidio was turned over to the National Park Service in 1994. Its 1480 acres are filled with nature, history and buildings left over from its military days (including a bowling alley!). The Presidio is home to Fort Point, the scenic 3-mile **Golden Gate Promenade** trail, the graceful **Palace of Fine Arts** and San Francisco's favorite place to be naked, beautiful **Baker Beach** (Gibson Rd).

☎ 415-561-4323; W www.nps.gov/prsf

THE CLIFF HOUSE & SUTRO BATHS

Overlooking broad and beautiful Ocean Beach, the Cliff House complex is undergoing a renovation, which should be complete by mid-2004. The restaurant and bar remain open during construction; the food is unexciting, but the view of the ocean (especially at sunset!) is unbeatable. The complex overlooks **Seal Rock** and the ruins of the once-opulent 19th-century **Sutro Baths**; the crumbling remains give the beach a ghostlike feel. Behind the restaurant is the **Camera Obscura** (☎ 415-750-0415; admission $1; open 11am-sunset), a neat Victorian projection device.

☎ 415-386-3330; W www.cliffhouse.com; 1090 Point Lobos Ave

GOLDEN GATE PARK

The park's too big to explore fully, but check out the **Japanese Tea Garden** (adult/child $2/1; open 9am-6pm), with very Zen roses and perfect green tea; the **California Academy of Sciences** (☎ 415-750-7145; W www.cal academy.org; adult/child $10/7; open 9am-6pm), a collection of quality natural history displays; and **Stowe Lake Boathouse** (☎ 415-752-0347; boats $13-16/hr; open 10am-4pm), where you can paddle with someone special.

☎ 415-831-2700; free (some attractions charge admission); open sunrise-sunset

PALACE OF THE LEGION OF HONOR

The Legion of Honor is a work of art in itself, a beaux arts confection overlooking Land's End and the Golden Gate Bridge. The collection of ancient and European art is worth the trip, especially the huge Rodin selection.

☎ 415-863-3330; W www.thinker.org; 34th Ave, north of Clement; adult/child $8/6; open 9:30am-5pm Tue-Sun

FORT FUNSTON

It's a dog park (leashes required), a nude beach, a fort, a hang-gliding launch and the trailhead for popular 1-mile **Fort Funston Sunset Trail** and more difficult 3-mile **Coastal Trail**. Follow the Great Hwy south and make a right on Skyline Blvd; the park is just past Lake Merced.

☎ 415-556-8371; open 6am-9pm

SLEEPING

San Francisco accommodations are notoriously pricey. The best bet for road-trippers is to stay on 101 after crossing the Golden Gate Bridge, follow it through the Presidio and out onto Lombard St, which is lined with moderately priced old-fashioned motels. Or call **Topaz Hotel Services** (☎ *510-628-4440, 800-677-1550;* w *www.hotelres.com)* for more options.

HI-SAN FRANCISCO FISHERMAN'S WHARF
This converted barracks at Fort Mason (near Fisherman's Wharf) has 150 beds in various arrangements, plus a kitchen, dining room and lounge areas.

☎ 415-771-7277; w www.norcalhostels.org; Bldg 240 McDowell Ave; dorm beds $22-29, rooms $67.50-73.50

GOLDEN GATE CITY MOTEL
This inexpensive, basic motel is just a block from the Presidio gate.

☎ 415-567-2425; 2707 Lombard St; singles/doubles $55-95

MARINA MOTEL
The standout on Lombard St is this family-owned motel with a secluded courtyard. Built in 1939, it has retained some of its vintage motor court charm.

☎ 415-921-9406; w www.marinamotel.com; singles/doubles $85-149

ROBERTS-AT-THE-BEACH MOTEL
Sleep by the sea at this less-than-luxurious but clean budget choice.

☎ 415-564-2610; 2828 Sloat Blvd; rooms start at $70

SEAL ROCK INN
Overlooking the beach, this older hotel is convenient to Hwy 1 and advance reservations can get you a full kitchen or fireplace.

☎ 415-752-8000; w www.sealrockinn.com; 545 Point Lobos Ave; rooms start at $90/120 winter/summer

EATING

Check the free weeklies for more listings of this city's celebrated cuisine; the choices listed here are all close to Hwy 1.

BEACH CHALET BREWERY & RESTAURANT
Housed on the 2nd floor of a beautifully restored 1925 beachfront building, this spacious brewpub serves several house-made brews and a sizeable food menu. Large windows face Ocean Beach, and the sunset views alone are worth the visit.

☎ 415-386-8439; 1000 Great Hwy

LOUIS' RESTAURANT
Right behind the Cliff House, this packed and pleasant diner has a great open-faced roast beef sandwich and better view.

☎ 415-387-6330; 902 Point Lobos; meals $5-13; open 6:30am-4:30pm Mon-Fri, 6:30am-6pm

ANGKOR WAT
Great Cambodian cuisine comes with a bonus: The Cambodian Royal Ballet performs here on Friday and Saturday night.

☎ 415-221-7887; 4217 Geary Blvd; entrees $6-15; open 11am-2:30pm & 5-10pm

PLUTO'S FRESH FOOD FOR A HUNGRY UNIVERSE
It's cheap, it's usually organic and it's got huge salads and meat-and-potato classics, all served amid classic sci-fi decor.

☎ 415-753-8867; 627 Irving St; entrees $3-7; open 11:30am-10pm

EBISU

Settle down on traditional Japanese tatamis for some of the city's best sushi, tempura and noodle dishes.

☎ 415-566-1770; 1283 9th Ave; entrees $9-17; open 11:30am-2pm Mon-Fri, 5-10pm Mon-Wed, 5pm-midnight Thu-Fri, 11:30am-midnight Sat, 11:30am-10pm Sun

THE GANGES

Near Golden Gate Park, this vegetarian restaurant has pillows on the floor and a highly recommended chana masala (garbanzo bean and mushroom curry).

☎ 415-661-7290; 775 Frederick St; entrees $3-16; open 5-10pm Tue-Sun

ENTERTAINMENT

Hedonism has been part of this town's DNA since the gold rush, so the range of ways one can entertain oneself here is not surprising. Upscale cocktail lounges, neighborhood dives, trance clubs, live music venues, transvestite bars – you name it, it's here. There's high culture too – a world-class symphony, avant-garde theater, highbrow cinema and inventive modern dance companies. Nightlife centers include the **Mission**, the **Castro**, **South of Market** and **North Beach**. Our recommendation: Leaf through the free weeklies to see what's on, park the car and take **MUNI** (☎ 415-673-6864; w www.sfmuni.com; tickets $1) to your venue of choice, as parking is near impossible. MUNI operates buses, light rail, streetcars and the famed cable cars, and offers late-night 'Owl' service on some lines. Check the website for route maps and schedules.

STAYING A WHILE?

We've limited ourselves to the coast, but if you're going to stick around for a while, here are a few must-sees:

San Francisco Museum of Modern Art (☎ 415-357-4000; w www.sfmoma.com; 151 3rd St) Eclectic, iconic and outrageous aesthetics

Chinatown (cnr Grant & Bush Sts) Culture, kitsch and dim sum

Mission Dolores (☎ 415-621-8203; 3321 16th St) The old adobe heart of San Francisco

Cable Cars (☎ 415-673-6864; w www.sfmuni.com) A national monument you can ride!

Fisherman's Wharf (☎ 415-626-7070; waterfront from Grant to Van Ness Aves) A million tourists can't be wrong

Alcatraz (☎ 415-705-5555; w www.blueandgoldfleet.com; piers 39 & 41) California's most photogenic prison

Pac Bell Park (☎ 415-979-2400; w www.sfgiants.com; 24 Willie Mays Plaza) A guaranteed home run

The Castro (Castro St btwn Market St & 20th, Market btwn Church & Castro Sts) The city's gay heartland

The Haight (Haight St btwn Masonic & Stanyan) Where the Summer of Love lives on

On the Road

South of San Francisco, Hwy 1 passes through decidedly less scenic **Daly City**. This bland, residential suburb of tiny, colored houses served as the inspiration for the '60s tune 'Little Boxes' ('made of ticky-tacky'). Soon, however, the Pacific Ocean fills the panorama.

Pacifica (population 45,000) is a seaside sprawler with a pre-fab downtown centered on Rockaway Beach Ave, with a few hotels and dining options. Friday nights are special at **Sea Bowl** (☎ 650-738-8190; 3625 Hwy 1; bowling $8/hr), when they combine bowling with hot music and a laser light show.

Watch erosion in motion at **Devil's Slide**, which actually drops mansions into the drink every winter.

Gray Whale Cove State Beach (admission $8) attracts nudists despite the hefty fee. **Montara State Beach**, farther south, is much nicer (and free); nudists also hang out.

Montara (population 2800) has a couple of interesting shops and hotels, plus the awesome **Point Montara Lighthouse & Hostel** (☎ 650-728-7177; 16th St; bunks $15-18, private rooms $52) in an 1875 lighthouse.

Follow the signs to **Moss Beach Distillery** (☎ 650-728-5595; cnr Beach Way & Ocean Blvd; entrees $17-30; open noon-10pm Mon-Sat, 10am-10pm Sun), which served booze illegally during Prohibition and is now an official historic landmark.

Miramar (population 400) offers a few cozy businesses like **Ono Hawaiian Grill** (☎ 650-726-8114; 3048 N Cabrillo Hwy; entrees $8-12; open 11:30am-10pm), which serves great ribs.

San Mateo Coast

The nearby beaches – Dunes and Pillar Point – are legendary; this is where surfing champion Mark Foo met his match in 1994, an 18-footer that was by no means the largest wave in local history.

Half Moon Bay (population 11,000) is best known for the **Art & Pumpkin Festival** (w www.halfmoonbaychamber.org), held in mid-October so farmers can carve their Volkswagen-sized squash by Halloween. It's worth planning your vacation around.

The upscale town is pricey, but **Half Moon Bay State Beach** (☎ 650-726-8820; Kelly Ave; campsites $12) has the best views around. Much nicer accommodations can be arranged through the **B&B Information Line** (☎ 650-712-9466).

Top quality eateries are everywhere, but the queen of the strip is **Pasta Moon** (☎ 650-726-5125; 315 Main St; lunch $11-20, dinner $11-27; open 11:30am-10pm), worth the drive from San Francisco for the rock shrimp pizza.

If you'd rather sleep than explore pumpkin-themed gift shops, crash at **Cameron's Restaurant & Inn** (☎ 650-726-9613; w www.cameronsinn .com; 1410 S Cabrillo Hwy; rooms start at $89), a British-style roadhouse pub that includes a beer with your room.

Another good spot for a tipple is east of Hwy 1 on Hwy 84, at **San Gregorio General Store** (☎ 650-726-0565; Hwy 84; open 9am-6pm), with a full bar and live music (usually Irish rock) on weekend afternoons.

Also worth a short inland excursion is tiny **Pescadero** and its claim to fame, **Duarte's Tavern** (☎ 650-879-0464; 202 Stage Rd; diner food $5-15; open 7am-midnight), renowned for its apricot pie.

Why are there so many youth hostels in historic lighthouses? Who knows. Just book a bunk at **Pigeon Point Lighthouse** (☎ 650-879-0633; dorm beds $12-15, private rooms $52), with the best back porch anywhere.

Kids love **Año Nuevo State Reserve** (☎ 650-879-2025, 800-444-7275; w www.anonuevo.org; admission $5, seal walks $4) and its winter inhabitants: some 3000 very large, very loud elephant seals. Fierce 5000-pound males fight for the ladies in December, while pups are born in late January. Make reservations for guided seal walks in advance.

Across from the park, **Costanoa** (☎ 650-879-1100, 800-738-7477; w www.costanoa.com; 2001 Rossi Rd; rooms $205-240, cabins $70-175, tent/RV sites $30/40) is luxurious – the campsites have saunas.

Take Bonny Doon Rd northeast to the **Bonny Doon Vineyard Tasting Room** (☎ 831-425-4518; w www.bonnydoonvineyard.com; 10 Pine Flat Rd; open 11am-5pm), popular among folks who prefer a sense of humor with their favorite vintages.

Kids prefer **Wilder Ranch State Park** (☎ 831-426-0505; admission $3; open sunrise-sunset), with historic farmhouses and excellent hiking. Try the 4-mile **Eucalyptus Loop** during butterfly season or the 6-mile **Wilder Ridge Loop**, with incredible spring wildflowers.

Santa Cruz

POPULATION 55,000; MAP 3

If you're over art galleries and bored with B&Bs, rejoice! This is the bona fide beach town you (and your kids) have been waiting for. Santa Cruz is famous for strong surfing culture, and is home to over 13,000 left-of-center students at the University of California, Santa Cruz. The town has a sense of humor (the university's mascot is a banana slug), thrill rides and a fine selection of beaches. Bonus: Thanks to a trick of geography, it has the best weather on the Northern California coast.

SIGHTS & ACTIVITIES

SANTA CRUZ BEACH BOARDWALK

This 1906 boardwalk has everything you need: Cotton candy, those dastardly 'ring around the bottle' games and, of course, the half-mile-long Giant Dipper, an aging wooden roller coaster sure to squeeze a scream out of you.

☎ 831-423-5590; rides $1-4

SURFING MUSEUM

Dude – did you know that this was, like, the first surf spot in the continental USA? Check out the gnarly shark-bit board and lots of local lore at this totally awesome (if tiny) museum. Talkative old-timers spin suspect tales from 2pm to 4pm Fridays.

☎ 831-429-3429; W Cliff Dr; admission $2; open 10am-4pm Thu-Mon

THE MYSTERY SPOT

Most of your half-hour tour into the redwood-ringed heart of Santa Cruz's own personal twilight zone is dedicated to debunking the debunkers. Honestly, there really does seem to be something spooky going on around here. On this steeply sloping hillside, compasses point crazily, mysterious forces push you around and buildings lean at silly angles.

☎ 831-423-8897; 465 Mystery Spot Rd (3 miles north of town); adult/child $5/3; open 9am-5pm

GO SKATE

You've been cooped up in that car far too long. Why not rent a surfboard ($5/10 hr/day), body board ($3/10) or some inline skates ($5/15) and work out some of those road rage–inspired aggressions?

☎ 831-425-8578; 601 Beach St; open 9am-7pm

VENTURE QUEST

Take advantage of the protected water and fabulous sunshine by renting a kayak (singles/doubles $20/40 for 2 hrs), or booking a guided tour.

☎ 831-427-2267; W www.kayaksantacruz.com; 125 Beach St

STAGNARO'S SPORTFISHING

Hemingway fans and other armchair fishers, take note: This is your chance to live the dream on a 35-passenger boat, fishing for rock cod, salmon or albacore tuna. Shipping is available, or you can donate your catch to area food banks.

☎ 831-427-0230; W www.stagnaros.com; Municipal Wharf

SLEEPING

Summer weekends are overbooked and exorbitant; budget travelers should plan to visit midweek.

NEW BRIGHTON STATE BEACH

Make reservations well in advance for these blufftop sites overlooking the bay, just south of Santa Cruz in nearby Capitola. It's as lovely as a wilderness area gets this close to civilization.

☎ 800-444-7275; W www.reserveamerica.com; campsites $14

SANTA CRUZ KOA

For more modern camping facilities – hot water is always a big draw – head south 12 miles on Hwy 1 then east on San Andreas Rd. It's not that close to the urban action, which is exactly what campers here have in mind.

☎ 831-722-0551; 1186 San Andreas Rd; tent/RV sites $35/44

HI CARMELITA COTTAGES HOSTEL

It's clean, friendly, and just two blocks from the beach – so make reservations, or arrive by 5pm (when the office opens) and keep your fingers crossed.

☎ 831-423-8304; 321 Main St; dorm beds $17/20 member/nonmember

FIRESIDE INN MOTEL

This clean, no-frills hotel, close to the beach, boardwalk and downtown, is representative of the 50 or so mid-range options in town.

☎ 831-426-7123; 311 Second St; rooms $100-200 summer, $40-100 winter

SEA & SAND INN

Rooms are cookie-cutter upscale, but what a view! Enjoy your complimentary full breakfast or evening wine-and-cheese overlooking the boardwalk.

☎ 831-427-3400; W www.santacruzmotels.com; 201 W Cliff Dr; rooms $159-359 summer, $129-269 winter

EATING

In the grand tradition of university towns, Santa Cruz cuisine is inexpensive, healthy and plentiful.

REBECCA'S MIGHTY MUFFINS

Carbo-loading is never a chore at this cozy coffee joint with huge muffins and other treats, plus packaged salads and sandwiches at lunch.

☎ 831-429-1940; 514A Front St; fresh-baked treats $3-6; open 7am-3pm Mon-Fri, 8am-5pm Sat-Sun

TAQUERIA VALLARTA

It's cheap, it's fast and it serves some of the best food in town; if you don't believe me, take a look at the lines out the door.

☎ 831-471-2655; 1101 Pacific Ave; Mexican fast food $4-10; open 11am-9pm

TOP SPOTS TO SUN YOUR BUNS

Though nude beaches abound in California, such exposure is technically forbidden. Keep your eyes out for police, as they occasionally enforce laws against public nudity.

Sculptured Beach: This Point Reyes standout has wild rock formations, but be careful of high tide.

Red Rock Beach: Just south of Stinson Beach, this cliffside spot is superior.

Baker Beach: Here's San Francisco's best place to show off.

Bonny Doon Beach: North of Santa Cruz, it's naturally shielded from the wind.

Andrew Molera State Park: This Big Sur standout also attracts vacationing families, so please be polite.

Pirate's Cove: San Luis Obispo lets it all hang out.

Gaviota State Park: North of Santa Barbara, it also has hot springs.

Point Dume: Malibu gets naked.

Abalone Cove: This Palos Verdes Peninsula gem is hard to find, but worth it.

ZACHARY'S

Santa Cruz's best hangover breakfast can be had at this cavernous downtown landmark; the homefries are tops, and Mike's Mess (recommended) makes them even better.

☎ 831-427-0646; 819 Pacific Ave; entrees $3-8; open 7am-2:30pm

SATURN CAFÉ

The burgers are fat and there's a killer vegetarian corn dog, but the late hours and hip decor – check out the rad tables – are the best reasons to come.

☎ 831-429-8505; 145 Laurel St; diner dishes $6-8; open 11:30am-3am Sun-Thu, 11:30am-4pm Fri-Sat

ENTERTAINMENT

Santa Cruz knows how to party. Pick up a copy of *Good Times* (**W** www.gdtimes.com) to find out what's on.

THE CATALYST

Mediocre deli by day and world-class music venue by night, it's more than just another bar: It's a tradition. Check online to see what's up.

☎ 831-423-1336; **W** www.catalystclub.com; 1011 Pacific Ave

KUUMBWA JAZZ CENTER

This cool bar is a relaxing place to imbibe even before local and international musicians cruise in to do their thing.

☎ 831-427-2227; 320 Cedar St

COCOANUT GROVE BALL ROOM

This refurbished big band hall doesn't do champagne music anymore – it's *the* top spot in town for Latin music, from salsa to hip hop. The dancing here is hot.

☎ 831-423-2053; 400 Beach St

NICKELODEON THEATRE

This isn't your average theater: During research, they were screening *Goonies* with Corey Feldman officiating, live and in person. Hell yeah.

☎ 831-426-7500; **W** www.thenick.com; 210 Lincoln St

SHAKESPEARE SANTA CRUZ

There's more to college than just partying. Check out UC thespians doing their thing at performances that may or may not have been written by the old bard.

☎ 831-459-2159; **W** www.shakespearesantacruz.com; 1156 High St; tickets $24-32 adult, $10-18 child

On the Road

Almost an extension of Santa Cruz, **Capitola** (population 12,000) wraps its exquisite stretch of coastline with a clutch of colorfully stuccoed knick-knack shops, expensive hotels and upscale beach bars.

Its claim to fame is the Sunday champagne brunch at **Shadowbrook** (*☎ 831-475-1511; 1750 Wharf Rd; dinner $13-28, other entrees $8-15; open 11:30am-9pm Mon-Sat, 10am-2:30pm & 4:30-9pm Sun*), where old-school gourmet (prime rib, crab omelets) still reigns supreme. Bonus: You descend to the dining room on a tram.

Most folks don't see much of **Aptos** (population 25,000) except popular **Seacliff State Beach** (*☎ 800-444-7275; **W** www.reserveamerica.com; tent/RV sites $21/24, day-use $3*), with a partially sunken WWI supply ship.

But there's a great town just past the strip malls, east on Soquel Dr and over the bridge – it's definitely worth exploring.

The best campsites around are at **Sunset State Beach** (☎ *800-444-7275;* [w] *www.reserveamerica.com; campsites $22),* where tree-sized drift-wood washes up onshore.

The next sizeable city is **Watsonville**, an agribusiness center and Mexican-American stronghold with several swank-free hotels and authentic taquerias. If you'd like to see the fields up close, drive to **Zmudowski State Beach**, which winds through organic and traditional farms to a truly lonely shore.

Beneath the POW flags, **J&S Surplus & Outdoor Store** (☎ *831-724-0588; cnr Hwy 1 & N Struve Rd; open 9am-6pm)* has camping equipment, paintball and hookups with a Watsonville firing range for those inter-ested in exercising their Second Amendment right.

Castroville (population 5000) hosts the **Artichoke Festival** ([w] *www .artichoke-festival.org)* in May, but stop into the **Giant Artichoke Restaurant** (☎ *831-633-3204; 11261 Merritt St; dishes $6-14)* any time.

Monterey

POPULATION 31,000; MAP 4

Spiritually, if not geographically, Monterey is the gateway to the Central California coastline. Instead of tie-dyed T-shirts, expect designer casual-wear. The mansions are appropriately ostentatious, fronted by gleaming SUVs, and restaurant-goers prefer cloth napkins and stemware with their pizza and burgers, thank you very much. Monterey is posh.

Even college communists from Santa Cruz can't fault the overprivi-leged for settling this stunning peninsula, however. Within a shoreline some religions consider irrefutable evidence of the divine are eucalyp-tus groves filled with monarch butterflies, one of the country's finest

---

PICK YOUR OWN IN WATSONVILLE

Watsonville is known for its growing attractions: Pick-your-own vegetables, flowers and fruits. Call ahead to check on the avail-ability of your favorites.

Royal Oaks Mushrooms (☎ *408-779-2362; 15480 Wat-sonville Rd)* does different shrooms year-round.

Emile Agaccio Farms (☎ *831-728-2009; cnr Casserly Rd & Hwy 152)* has strawberries, raspberries and Olallies April–July.

Privedelli Farm (831-724-9282; 375 Pioneer View) serves blackberries July–September, and dozens of apples and pears September–December.

Gizdich 'Pik-Yor-Sef' Ranch (831-722-2458; [w] *www .gizdichranch.com; 55 Peckham Rd)* features berries and apples, plus local wines, pies and cutesy kitsch.

Or, simply stop by one of the many roadside stands or the **Watsonville Certified Farmer's Market** (☎ *831-263-4000;*

aquariums, a festive tourist quarter with lovingly restored adobe buildings and a 17-mile drive to show it all off.

SIGHTS & ACTIVITIES

MONTEREY BAY AQUARIUM
This world-famous institute exhibits imaginative displays involving all sorts of aquatic life, from kelp forests to some seriously trippy jellyfish. Though the price is steep, your cash is going to salvage the oceans from uninformed overuse. Besides, you've got to see an otter feeding (10:30am, 1:30pm and 3:30pm) at least once in your life.

☎ 831-648-4888; 886 Cannery Row; adult/child $18/9; open 10am-6pm

CANNERY ROW
Handmade fudge and souvenir T-shirts are just the tip of the iceberg: Real tourist-trap aficionados will want to indulge themselves with **Steinbeck's Spirit of Monterey Wax Museum** (☎ 831-375-1010; W www.wax-museum.com; adult/child $9/6; open 9am-9pm), where 'lifelike wax figures' portray Steinbeck-era Monterey.

PATH OF HISTORY
Old Monterey is home to an extraordinary assemblage of 19th-century brick and adobe buildings. Pick up a brochure (available everywhere) and wander the streets on your own, or meet your fellow historians at the **Maritime Museum** (☎ 831-373-2469; Custom House Plaza; adult/child $6/4; open 10am-5pm) for a guided tour.

☎ 831-649-7118; Custom House Plaza

17-MILE DRIVE
You'll pay $8 to drive through this admittedly lovely gated community, where you can see millionaires in their natural habitat. The spectacular drive follows the rocky shore and winds through Pebble Beach, home of the famed golf course. Enter through any of five gates; the folks at the **Monterey Visitors Center** (☎ 831-649-1770; 5 Custom House Plaza; open 10am-5pm) can point you in the right direction.

HIKING & BIKING
Stretch your legs on the 3-mile **Asilomar Trail**, following amazing coastline from Asilomar Conference Center on Sunset Dr. The **Monterey Peninsula Recreational Trail,** popular among bicyclists and hikers, begins behind **Bay Bikes Bicycle Rentals** (☎ 831-646-9090; 640 Wave St) on Cannery Row.

MONTEREY BAY KAYAKS
Explore the Monterey Bay National Marine Sanctuary in a rented kayak ($30/day); you can also arrange three-hour guided tours ($55).

☎ 831-373-5357; 693 Del Monte Ave; open 9am-6pm

SLEEPING

Budget hotels congregate north of the Fremont St exit off Hwy 1, running anywhere between $30 to $50 on winter weekdays and $60 to $200 on sunny summer weekends.

LAGUNA SECA RECREATION AREA
Nine miles east of Monterey, this private campsite, next to Laguna Seca Raceway (don't bother on race day), has a fishing pond and shooting range.

☎ 831-755-4899, 888-588-2267; Hwy 68; tent/RV sites $22/24

MONTEREY HOSTEL
This new HI entry is well-located (just four blocks from the aquarium) and is sure to earn four stars from the budget backpacker crowd.

☎ 831-649-0375; W montereyhostel.com; 778 Hawthorn St; dorm beds $21/16 adult/child; private room $54

THE MONTEREY HOTEL
This splendid luxury property, resplendent in floral prints, features smallish standard rooms, stunning 'living areas' and top-notch service.

☎ 831-375-3184; W www.montereyhotel.com; 406 Alvarado St; rooms $139-299

OLD MONTEREY INN
You've got to love an innkeeper who relishes the job of transforming a humble B&B into a cozy slice of heaven. Sure, you pay for perfection, but with gardens, great rooms and a big breakfast to start your day, why not?

☎ 831-375-8284, 800-350-2344; 500 Martin St; rooms start at $230

EATING

OLD MONTEREY BAY CAFÉ
This place is kinder to your wallet than to your arteries. Soups and burgers are fine, and breakfast served all day keeps the hangovers away.

☎ 831-646-1021; 489 Alvarado St; entrees $5-12; open 7am-2:30pm

PARIS BAKERY
Even neurotic trophy spouses will go off their diets at this buttery bakery, with both sweet and savory delights.

☎ 831-646-1620; 271 Bonifacio Plaza; baked goods $3-5; open 6am-6:30pm

SIAMESE BAY RESTAURANT
It's been voted the best Thai food on the peninsula several times, and the $6 lunch buffet makes it the best deal in town.

☎ 831-373-1550; 131 Webster St; lunch $6, dinner $9-16; open 11:30am-2:30pm Mon-Fri, 5-10pm daily

THE FISHWIFE
You'll get far better seafood here than at plenty of places charging twice as much. Don't miss the calamari or Key lime pie.

☎ 831-375-7107; 1996½ Sunset Dr; lunch $7-10, dinner $8-15; open 11:30am-9pm

SARDINE FACTORY
There are folks too cool for most of Cannery Row, but no one turns down a meal at the Sardine Factory. Make reservations, dress to impress and expect some of the best (if overpriced) seafood around.

☎ 831-373-3775; 701 Wave St; dinner $28-40; open 5-10pm

ENTERTAINMENT

Most of the after-dark activity centers on Alvarado St. Pick up a copy of the free *Coast Weekly* (W www.coastweekly.com) to see what's on.

THE MUCKY DUCK
This somewhat authentic English pub packs in the partiers on weekends with live music and a wide selection of beer and single-malt scotches. Smokers gravitate to the garden patio.

☎ 831-655-3031; 479 Alvarado St

PLANET GEMINI
This is the hottest spot for Latin dance and hip hop in town – well, on Cannery Row, anyway. There's sometimes a cover for live music.

☎ 831-373-1449; 625 Cannery Row

SLY McFLY'S JAZZ & BLUES DINNER HOUSE
The bar is relaxed, the food – burgers are recommended – is good, and the calendar of live music is absolutely outstanding. There's often a cover for shows.

☎ 831-372-3225; 700-A Cannery Row; entrees $7-17

Carmel-By-The-Sea

POPULATION 4500; MAP 4

Connected to Monterey by both Hwy 1 and the 17-Mile Drive, this former art colony is even wealthier and more exclusive, while still proudly showcasing its bohemian heritage. And it isn't just the galleries: Carmel continues to resist the tyranny of big government by refusing to use street addresses. The hamlet's main claim to fame, however, is having elected actor Clint Eastwood as mayor. Attractions include a neat grid of picturesque homes, an impressive coastal frontage and an upscale shopping street (no chewing gum or ice cream allowed!).

SIGHTS & ACTIVITIES

Shopping is the favorite sport of most Carmel visitors – careful with that credit card!

CARMEL CITY BEACH PARK

This is one swath of sand worth digging your toes into – sliced from the forest and flanked by cypress trees, it's one of the prettiest city beaches in California.

☎ 831-624-3543; Ocean Ave; open sunrise-10pm

MISSION SAN CARLOS BORROMÉO DE CARMELO

Perhaps the most photogenic of all the missions, the riverside chapel boasts a great museum and is the final resting place of Father Junipero Serra, who founded 21 California missions and died here in 1784.

☎ 831-624-1271; 3080 Rio Rd; adult/child $2/1 donation; open 9:30am-4:30pm

GALLERY WALKS

With more than 60 art galleries and studios open for business, most in the downtown square bounded by 5th and 7th Aves, Lincoln St and Mission St, Carmel keeps plenty of artists from starving. Grab a **Gallery Guide** or just explore.

SLEEPING & EATING

This is a B&B sort of town; contact **Monterey Peninsula Reservations** (☎ 831-655-3487, 888-655-3424; w www.monterey-reservations.com) for information on lots of them.

MONTEREY BAY NATIONAL MARINE SANCTUARY

Look toward the sunset to see one of California's most impressive protected spaces, the **Monterey Bay National Marine Sanctuary** (w montereybay.nos.noaa.gov; 299 Foam St, Monterey, CA 93940).

Occupying 5300 square miles and larger than some states, it's home to more than 25 endangered species, the 10,000-foot-deep Monterey Canyon, and lots of very cute sea otters who hang out around the kelp forests (incidentally, the nation's largest) in Monterey Bay.

Government protection basically means that plants and animals are closely monitored, while certain activities – for instance, drilling for oil – are forbidden. Tourism is encouraged, however, and the diving and kayaking opportunities are magnificent.

SADDLE MOUNTAIN RECREATION PARK

Five miles east of Carmel, along the Carmel River, this pleasant private campsite has lots of amenities, including a small video arcade.

☎ 831-624-1617; Carmel Valley Rd; campsites $28-42

THE HOMESTEAD

With comfy cottages and a perfect downtown location, this is a great deal.

☎ 831-624-4119; cnr Lincoln St & 8th Ave; rooms $85-140

CANDLE LIGHT INN

This friendly inn is run by a French woman with loads of advice on top restaurants. The rooms are snug and comfortable, and, as a special touch, continental breakfast is left outside your room in a basket.

☎ 831-624-6451; San Carlos St btwn 4th & 5th Aves; rooms $119-209

JACK LONDON'S

Big burgers and sandwiches are paired with microbrews at this casual watering hole, tucked into an alley off San Carlos St. Cocktails are also available.

☎ 831-626-2336; San Carlos St btwn 5th & 6th Aves; entrees $7-15

THE GEM

European classics – frog legs Provençale, beef Wellington – are prepared to California specs (read: less butter) and served up right in this bright bistro.

☎ 831-625-4367; San Carlos St btwn Ocean & 7th Aves; entrees $15-25; open 5-9pm

PORTA BELLA

If you're going to splurge, do it right: Porta Bella is charming, it's got outdoor seating, the wine list rocks and the Mediterranean cuisine is sure to impress.

☎ 831-624-4395; Ocean Ave btwn Lincoln & Monte Verde Sts; entrees $22-65; open 11:30am-10pm (bar open till midnight)

On the Road

South of Carmel, gorgeous **Point Lobos State Reserve** *(☎ 831-624-4909; Hwy 1; admission $6; open 9am-7pm)* is so popular that a strict 450-person limit can keep you waiting for hours. The rugged, 6-mile **Point Lobos Perimeter Trail**, featuring seal pups in spring, is worth the wait.

MONARCH BUTTERFLIES

They're tiny but tough, flying an annual migratory pattern that rivals that of many birds, often more than 100 miles per day at 10,000 feet or higher. The luckiest end up along the Central Coast, and the Monterey Peninsula sees plenty.

The orange-and-black butterflies aren't as ostentatious as you'd expect; look for clusters of brownish-looking leaves toward the top of eucalyptus trees. Those are the butterflies, and it's against the law to disturb them.

Every winter, millions of monarchs take up residence in the eucalyptus trees at George Washington Park in Monterey, and at Monarch Grove Sanctuary in Pacific Grove. Some other top spots for wintering monarchs include Natural Bridges State Park in Santa Cruz, Pismo Beach and San Simeon Natural Preserve near Hearst Castle.

Locals, however, head south to **Garrapata State Park** (☎ 831-667-2315; admission free), with 4 miles of wild coastline and lots of great hiking – without all the tourists.

Big Sur

POPULATION 1300; MAP 5

Though its boundaries aren't clearly defined, you'll find Big Sur at the wild heart of Hwy 1, where the mountains, traded off in leagues between desert and rainforest, need no mediator in meeting the sea.

Plan ahead for this 90-mile, at least five-hour drive: Gas, film and food along this stretch cost almost twice what they do at either end. Pick up a free copy of *El Sur Grande* (**W** www.bigsurcalifornia.org) for up-to-date information on trails and campsites.

Posh roadhouses are the rule, with room, board and often entertainment tucked into a single perfect crease in the mountains. They don't cater to budget travelers, however, who'll either camp or hold out until San Simeon.

Prepare yourself for a series of transcendental moments along this stretch of dramatic coastline. Its raw beauty is awe-inspiring, and when the sun goes down, the moon and the stars are the only streetlights.

LIGHTSTATION STATE HISTORIC PARK
You can visit this 1887 lightstation atop a giant moro rock formation only on a pre-arranged three-hour tour. It's worth it and – for ghost story fans – docents also offer special 'moonlight tours' on summer evenings.

☎ 831-625-4419; **W** www.lighthouse-pointsur-ca.org; tours 10am & 2pm Sat, 10am Sun, reservations required; adult/child $5/3

ANDREW MOLERA STATE PARK
It's only a few hundred feet to the picturesque, primitive campsites, but you can get a real workout on the lush and occasionally precipitous, 8-mile **Molera State Park Loop**, or take it easy on the gentle, 3-mile **Molera Point Trail**. Tidepooling, nude sunbathing and otter spotting are always popular, and **Molera Horseback Tours** (☎ 831-625-5486, 800-942-5486; **W** *www.molera horsebacktours.com; guided rides $25-60)* offers rides into the interior.

☎ 831-667-2315; Hwy 1; walk-in tent sites $3; open sunrise-sunset

BIG SUR RIVER INN
Relax by the river, swim in the pool or just enjoy the view; there's also a grocery store selling raingear and dry goods and an attached restaurant/deli *(entrees $8-14; open 9am-9pm)* that prides itself on its ribs.

☎ 831-667-2700; **W** www.bigsurriverinn.com; Hwy 1; rooms with/without view $85/170 winter, $125/225 summer

RIPPLEWOOD RESORT
Not particularly rustic cabins come with kitchenettes; there's a small market (with decent produce – a bonus) and small cafe, open for breakfast and lunch.

☎ 831-667-2242; **W** www.ripplewoodresort.com; cabins $100-120

FERNWOOD RESORT & CAMPGROUNDS
This superb campsite boasts an albino redwood tree (pretty weird) and restaurant with live music on weekends, when there's also a $10 barbecue.

☎ 831-667-2422; Hwy 1; walk-in/drive-in sites $8/27, rooms $47-111, entrees $7-18; restaurant open 3-9pm Mon-Thu, 11am-9pm Fri-Sun, bar open till 2am

PFEIFFER BIG SUR STATE PARK
Perhaps Big Sur's crown jewel, this beautiful state park has a fabulous collection of trails, including the pleasant 1-mile walk through the redwoods to **Pfeiffer**

Falls, the steep and scenic **Buzzard's Roost** loop, and the 10-mile **Pine Valley Trail** overnight hike into the Santa Lucia Mountains. There's even a beach with sea caves: Head 2 miles west on Sycamore Canyon Rd (unsigned; look for a paved road heading west).

The park also has some of the prettiest drive-in campsites around, plus the first-class 1930 **Big Sur Lodge** (☎ 800-424-4787; [W] *www.bigsurlodge.com; rooms $89-139 winter, $169-219 summer*), which boasts a respected fine dining restaurant. Just south, **Big Sur Ranger Station** *(open 8am-4pm)* has maps and helpful rangers.

☎ 800-444-7275; [W] www.reserveamerica.com; campsites $26, day-use $4

VENTANA INN, SPA & CAMPGROUND
This is where supermodels and CEOs get back to nature, with rooms, not camp-sites, a Japanese-style bath house, evening wine tastings and **Cielo Restaurant** *(Mediterranean-fusion cuisine $12-52; open noon-3pm & 6-9pm)*.

☎ 831-667-2331, 800-628-6588; [W] www.ventanainn.com; Hwy 1; campsites $30-40, rooms $300-900

NEPENTHE
A road-trip tradition since 1949, no Hwy 1 cruise is complete without a burger and brew, or surf and turf, atop this architectural marvel. The prices aren't as steep as the coastline, which dominates one of the best views in Big Sur.

☎ 831-667-2345; Hwy 1; lunch $9-15, dinner $12-39; open 11:30am-10pm

HENRY MILLER LIBRARY
The author lived and worked here from 1944 to 1962, and today Miller's shanty is a bookstore, art gallery and performance space hung with his eternal admon-ishment, 'Let us do our best, even if it gets us nowhere.' Nowhere still seems to attract artsy types who screen indy films and throw carnival-style parties here. Check the website.

☎ 831-667-2574; [W] www.henrymiller.org; donations appreciated; open 11am-6pm Wed-Mon and for special events

DEETJEN'S BIG SUR INN
Just south of the Henry Miller Library, this highly recommended overnight offers rustic Norwegian cabins and the requisite gourmet restaurant – breakfast is a deal.

☎ 831-667-2377; [W] www.deetjens.com; 48865 Hwy 1; rooms with private/shared bath $75/110 low, $90/180 high, breakfast $6-8, dinner $17-29; restaurant open 8am-noon & 6-8:30pm

PARTINGTON COVE
Descend the unofficial but obvious fire road along Partington Creek to this very cool cove, where pirates and, later, Prohibition-era bootleggers stashed their booty in a 110-foot-long tunnel. The beach is nice, too.

JULIA PFEIFFER BURNS STATE PARK
It's Big Sur's best photo op: Follow the half-mile **McWay Falls Overlook** trail to watch the waterfall drop 80 postcard-perfect feet into the open ocean. Stop and snorkel or continue along the 4-mile **Ewoldsen Loop** trail.

☎ 831-667-2315, reservations ☎ 800-444-7275; [W] www.reserveamerica.com; tent sites $18, day-use $6

ESALEN INSTITUTE
Revered by spiritual types who have learned to accept material abundance as a divine gift of the universe (read: rich hippies), Esalen is known for its top-notch classes covering everything from tantric sex to natural capitalism. If they have rooms open, they'll let you rent one and use their newly rebuilt sulfur hot springs on a cliff overlooking the ocean. Reservations required.

☎ 831-667-3000; [W] www.esalen.org; Hwy 1; dorm beds $90-105, rooms $130-170

THE MISSION TRAIL

From the late 1760s until the early 1780s, Father Junipéro Serra and his Catholic compatriots were on a mission: to meet the Spanish government's rather secular goal of founding a string of churches along the wild California coastline. These would beef up property claims against the encroaching European powers, convince various Indian tribes that morality lies in hard work, and (of course) celebrate the glory of God.

Padre Serra proved the man for the job. In 20 years he founded 20 missions along El Camino Real (today traced by Hwy 101), a record no one else could touch. Spain would go on to lose the territory to a rebellious Mexico shortly thereafter, but the missions remained.

Today the churches are symbols not only of Father Serra's mission, but of a conquest some call genocide. Mortality among the native workforce approached 80 percent, and entire cultures – their languages, art and science – were all but lost in the span of a single human lifetime. On a brighter note, Father Serra also brought the first grape cuttings to the region, basically founding the California wine industry.

Only a few of the missions are easily accessible from Hwy 1; but you'd still do well to pick just a few and save more time for the beach.

San Rafael Arcángel (1817): Father Vincente de Sarria founded this, one of the last missions, as a hospital for Indians ill with European diseases.

San Francisco de Asís (1776): San Francisco's centerpiece is surrounded with hot bars, cool restaurants and great murals.

Santa Cruz (1791): Bad karma (a high Native death toll) and half-hearted restoration make this one to skip.

San Carlos Borroméo de Carmelo (1770): Photo ops abound at this picturesque spot in Carmel.

San Miguel Arcángel (1797): Average and, in Paso Robles, a bit out of the way.

San Luis Obispo de Tolosa (1772): Beautiful to begin with, plus bonus Chumash art.

La Purísima Concepción (1787): The mission, near Lompoc, is just OK, but the hiking is great.

Santa Inés (1804): Not at all Danish, Solvang's mission has a cool collection of artifacts.

Santa Barbara (1786): It didn't get the 'Queen of the Missions' title for nothing.

San Buenaventura (1782): This one, in Ventura, is pleasant enough, but not spectacular.

San Juan Capistrano (1776): It's so pretty that the swallows return every year.

LIMEKILN STATE PARK

This new and still relatively uncrowded park has excellent campsites along a redwood-forested gorge, a very pretty beach, and a 2-mile **Nature Trail** through the forest to four large limekilns, built in 1887.

☎ 831-625-4419, reservations ☎ 800-444-7275; W www.reserveamerica .com; campsites $12, day-use $3

NEW CAMALDOLI HERMITAGE

Rooms at this self-sufficient community of Benedictine monks are often reserved up to six months in advance, but drop by anyway for liturgical worship or to pick up one of their handmade fruitcakes ($22).

☎ 831-667-2456; W www.contemplation.com; lodge/trailer hermitages $60/70 suggested donation

PLASKETT CREEK CAMPGROUND & BEACHES

This is one of Big Sur's most heavily used campgrounds. Across Hwy 1 are two of Big Sur's true gems: **Sand Dollar Beach** boasts the widest swath of sand, while **Jade Cove** is often carpeted with the semi-precious stones.

☎ 831-385-5434; Hwy 1; campsites $18

San Simeon

POPULATION 500; MAP 5

Budget travelers can finally afford a room and meal, but this former whaling station is more than just a service town. San Simeon and the castle looming above it are the enduring monuments to newspaper magnate William Randolph Hearst, inspiration for the movie *Citizen Kane*.

SIGHTS & ACTIVITIES

HEARST CASTLE

Keep in mind that this place was built by a guy who boasted (and there's evidence to back this up) that he started the Spanish-American war just to sell

---

DETOUR: TASSAJARA ZEN MOUNTAIN MONASTERY

The first Soto Zen monastery outside Japan was founded here, around these Santa Lucia hot springs, some 40 years ago. Today, **Tassajara** (☎ 415-863-3136, 831-659-2229; W www.sfzc.com/ Pages/Tassajara/Tassajara_Controls/zmc.html; open May-Sep only) still runs 5-day workshops (usually $300) during the summer 'Guest Season,' on everything from meditation to wildcrafting.

Folks uninterested in enlightenment can still stay here (yurt $160-260, dorm bed $80-95), including full access to the springs, while budget soakers can opt for day-use only (adult/ child $20/10, food not included) and pitch a tent just up the road at White Oaks or China Camp (☎ 831-385-5434; Tassajara Rd/CR 5007; primitive sites $7).

China Camp is also the trailhead of stunning 10-mile Pine Valley Trail, which runs through the Ventana Wilderness to Big Sur, and accesses wild hot springs en route.

---

newspapers. *La Cuesta Encantada*, as no one but Hearst ever called it, features 127 acres of gardens (most of the 90-species zoo has disbanded), 165 rooms, 61 *bathrooms*, Spanish cathedral ceilings, ancient Egyptian artifacts, Renaissance paintings and the best indoor pool anywhere. It's California's Graceland.

There are four main tours plus evening and holiday options; all will blow your mind. If it's your first time, however, just make sure to see the Roman Pool. Seriously.

☎ 800-445-4445; w www.hearstcastle.com; tours $10-14 adult, $5-7 child; open 8am-3:20pm

ELEPHANT SEALS
The **Friends of the Elephant Seals** has an office downtown, or just head 7.7 miles north to Piedras Blancas Vista Point, where elephant seals carouse almost year round. Volunteers are often available for tours.

☎ 805-924-1628; 250 San Simeon Ave, suite B; open 9:30am-5pm Mon-Fri

SLEEPING & EATING

SAN SIMEON STATE PARK
Both campsites are wonderful: The **San Simeon** section is protected and has hot showers, but waking up atop **Washburn** with the Pacific glittering beneath you…well, sometimes that's worth the chill.

☎ 805-927-2035; Washburn campsites $7, San Simeon campsites $12

SAN SIMEON LODGE
Of the hotels on the east side of Hwy 1 (which are about 20 percent cheaper than those on the west side), this has the easiest beach access, plus good, clean rooms.

☎ 805-927-4601; 9520 Castillo Dr; rooms start at $35/115 low/high season

SEBASTIAN'S STORE
If you're visiting **William Randolph Hearst Memorial Beach** and the fishing pier nearby, stop in to the 1852 store with a coffee shop, post office and the finest souvenirs in town.

ROBIN'S RESTAURANT
Locals love Robin's, and recommend the inspired vegetarian dishes (many with Asian overtones) as well as the classic meaty meals.

☎ 805-927-5007; 4095 Burton Dr; entrees $10-15; open 5-9pm

EL CHORLITO
If the phrase 'real Hatch green chile' means anything to you, you're already parking at this homey New Mexican (*not* Mexican) restaurant. Anyone else with a taste for the fiery is welcome to stop in for a treat.

☎ 805-927-3872; 9155 Hearst Dr; entrees $8-14; open 11:30am-9pm

On the Road

San Simeon's far fairer Siamese twin, **Cambria** (population 5500), is a friendly and unpretentious beachside community that bills itself as an art colony, but functions as a working-class resort town. It's got better-than-average shops and galleries, plus all the restaurants you'd ever need.

Its pride and joy is **Moonstone Beach**, named for the shoreline shimmering with smoothly weathered jade, agate and quartz, fronted by the 2-mile **Leffingwell Landing Trail** plus scores of adorable hotels and B&Bs. The **Cambria Chamber of Commerce** (☎ *805-927-3624*; w *www.cambriachamber.com; 767 Main St; open 9am-5pm Mon-Fri, 10am-2pm Sat-Sun*) can find you a great room.

At the northern shore of heavily industrialized Estero Bay, Cayucos (population 3000) doesn't really cater to tourists, reason enough to grab a cheap hotel room and spend the day on a board from the **Surf Company** (☎ 805-995-1000; 95 Cayucos Dr; full surf package $50/day; open 9am-6pm).

Top off your day at the **Old Cayucos Tavern** (☎ 805-995-3209; 130 Ocean Ave; open 10-2am) with live music on weekends and a card room.

Just south of town is **Morro Strand State Beach** (☎ 805-772-8812, reservations ☎ 800-444-7275; w www.reserveamerica.com; campsites $12) with views of astounding **Morro Rock**, an imposing volcanic plug that you can drive right up to – but no climbing.

Morro Bay (population 10,000) has a genial tourist quarter – which seems permanently trapped in 1954 – right in the shadow of the rock. Fish-and-chips stands, budget hotels and shops hawking shell sculptures abound. The classic tourist outing involves taking a water taxi or kayak from **Kayak Horizons** (☎ 805-772-6444; 551 Embarcadero) across the bay to sandy and isolated **Morro Dunes Nature Preserve**.

Serious campers can head south 12 miles on Los Osos Valley Rd. **Montaña de Oro State Park** (☎ 805-772-8812, reservations ☎ 800-444-7275; w www.reserveamerica.com; campsites $8) encompasses 8400 acres on this almost abandoned peninsula, with more than 50 miles of hiking trails, sea caves and monarch butterflies. It's primitive – bring your own water.

You can either head back north to Hwy 1 in Morro Bay, or take Los Osos Valley Rd east, right into downtown SLO.

San Luis Obispo

POPULATION 40,000

SLO (bored teens insist on pronouncing it 'slow') is just about perfect: a colorful and strollable downtown, a large student population with excellent taste in music and cuisine, a very nice mission, flawless weather and fine accommodations.

Sure, everyone leaves their heart in San Francisco. But the truly discriminating traveler leaves her chewing gum in San Luis Obispo.

SIGHTS & ACTIVITIES

MISSION SAN LUIS OBISPO DE TOLOSA
This mission's claim to fame is the beautiful wooden ceiling, framed with beams hauled 40 miles from the mountains. There's a great onsite museum; Mass is held at 7am and 10:30am weekdays and several times on Sunday.

☎ 805-543-6850; donations appreciated; open 9am-5pm

FARMER'S MARKET
It's worth planning your visit around: Every Thursday evening, organic produce stands, barbecues and live music make grocery shopping merry.

Downtown Higuera St; open 6:30-9pm Thu

BUBBLEGUM ALLEY
Between 733 and 737 Higuera St is some public art anyone can appreciate – well, except folks with germ phobias. It's an alleyway covered with decades' worth of chewing gum, crystallized into fractals worthy of Jackson Pollock.

BAR HOPPING
Grab the free weekly New Times (w www.newtimes-slo.com) and see what's on – probably plenty. Hot spots at press time included The Graduate (805-541-0969; 990 Industrial Way); the **SLO Brewing Company** (☎ 805-543-1843; 1119 Garden

St), with live music, pool and microbrews; and the **Frog & Peach Pub** (☎ *805-595-3764; 728 Higuera St)*, a nice conversational bar.

SLEEPING & EATING

The SLO **Chamber of Commerce** (☎ *805-781-2777;* W *www.visitslo.com; 1039 Chorro St; open 10am-5pm)* has hotel listings and free phones.

HOSTEL OBISPO
This well maintained hostel, in a sweet Victorian just a few minutes' walk from downtown, offers a free sourdough pancake breakfast.

☎ 805-544-4678; W www.hostelobispo.com; 1617 Santa Rosa St; dorm beds $18/20 member/nonmember, private rooms $40-55

SAND SUITES & MOTEL
Representative of the cluster of inexpensive chains and clean independent hotels at the intersection of Monterey St and Hwy 1, this is a great overnight.

☎ 805-544-3529, 800-441-4657; 1930 Monterey St; rooms start at $60/80 low/high season

MADONNA INN
Pity the well-bred stuffed shirts who can't let themselves appreciate the wonder and beauty that is the Madonna Inn. From the ornate dining room hung with chandeliers and resplendent in pink-lemonade naugahyde, to rooms decorated to resemble caves and gardens, this is beauty for its own sake. Stop by, at least for a cup of coffee.

☎ 805-543-3000, 800-543-9666; W www.madonnainn.com; 100 Madonna Rd; rooms $140-330

LUISA'S PLACE
Enjoy the best breakfast in SLO, served at a wraparound Formica bar.

☎ 805-541-0227; 964 Higuera; diner delicacies $4-8; open 6am-3pm Fri-Wed, 6am-8pm Thu

San Luis Obispo

PLACES TO STAY
11 Hostel Obispo
12 Madonna Inn

PLACES TO EAT
2 Luisa's Place
5 SLO Brewing Co
7 Golden China Restaurant
9 China Bowl, Santa Veggie
10 Big Sky Cafe

OTHER
1 Mission San Luis Obispo de Toloso
3 San Luis Obispo Chamber of Commerce
4 Frog & Peach Pub
6 Mother's Tavern
8 Spike's

GOLDEN CHINA RESTAURANT

Is it just the best Chinese buffet in town, or is it the best on the Central Coast? Budget and vegetarian travelers rely on these places, and with tasty food for cheap (lunch/dinner $7/11), they'll be feeling fine.

☎ 805-543-7354; 685 Higuera St; open 11:30am-9:30pm

SMOKIN' MOE'S BBQ

Get your pork, beef or poultry slow cooked and served up in portions that run from big to mammoth. Ribs are the specialty, but there are folks who come here just for the fried green tomatoes.

☎ 805-544-6193; 970 Higuera St; entrees $6-19; open 11am-9pm

BIG SKY CAFE

It's at the heart of town and loved for its inventive and inexpensive eats, made from local and seasonal food – fish from the bay, veggies from the valley, wines from the Central Coast. A must.

☎ 805-845-5401; 1121 Broad St; entrees $6-18; open 7am-10pm

On the Road

You'll exit SLO quickly, when Hwy 1 joins businesslike Hwy 101 for a brief, multi-lane stretch. Or, jump off the freeway and head west on Avila Beach Drive; as Morro Rock may have reminded you, this is volcano country – and that means hot springs.

Tasteful and elegant **Sycamore Mineral Springs** (☎ *805-595-7302;* W *www.sycamoresprings.com; 1215 Avila Beach Dr; rooms $140-406)* is an 1887 resort with private wooden hot tubs (non-guests $13/hr; open 24hrs) and an upscale restaurant.

Or indulge in the same healing waters just down the road (and scale) at **Avila Valley Hot Springs** (☎ *805-595-2359;* W *www.avilahot springs.com; 250 Avila Beach Dr; tent/RV sites $30/43, day-use $8; open 8am-9pm),* where you can soak all day in the big cement pool, or get a combo deal (includes soda and a slice of pizza) for just $11, then pitch your tent.

Continue past creepy Avila Beach to **Port San Luis**, gateway to Diablo Canyon Nuclear Plant and home of the fabulous **Fat Cats Café** (☎ *805-595-2204; diner dishes $5-14; open 24hrs),* where you can munch excellent onion rings and watch the fishing boats unload. Afterwards, head east on Cove Landing Rd to **Pirate's Cove Beach**, the nicest stretch of sand around, and clothing-optional to boot.

Jump back on Hwy 101 South toward beautiful **Pismo Beach** (population 8000), a low-key, low-maintenance paradise, with a broad, sandy beach, bronzed bums and bunnies, and excellent surfing.

The famous Pismo clams are generally off-limits (overclamming has taken its toll) but other, lesser clams are available at half a dozen chowder shops on the strip: **Splash Cafe** (☎ *805-773-4653; 197 Pomeroy Ln; fast food $2-6; open 10am-9pm)* can hook you up cheap.

North Beach Campground (☎ *800-444-7275;* W *www.reserveamerica .com; campsites $12)* has sand dunes and, in winter, millions of monarch butterflies.

Just south of town is truly awesome **Oceano Dunes Vehicular Recreation Area** (☎ *805-473-7220, reservations* ☎ *800-444-7275;* W *www.reserveamerica.com; campsites $6, day-use $4),* the only California beach open to ATVs. **BJ's ATV Rental** (☎ *805-481-5411; 197 Grand Ave)* rents the delightful little monsters for around $30 to $50 per hour, $135 to $250 per day. Campsites are more convenient than spectacular.

South of Pismo Beach, Hwy 1 separates from Hwy 101 and snakes inland across Santa Ynez Valley, actually a broad peninsula checkered with successful agribusinesses – think industrial chemicals, migrant farmworkers and *excellent* vegetable stands.

The friendly town of **Guadalupe** has a well-preserved art deco downtown and lots of delicious-smelling taquerias and panderias (sweetbread shops) that provide ample excuse for exploration.

You can't access most of this coast, as Vandenburg Air Force Base has reserved that primo property for itself – national security and all that. But you can visit **Lompoc** (pronounced lom-POKE; population 45,000) and its enormous collection of supermarkets and convenience stores.

It's not exactly a resort town, but does have **Mission la Purísima Concepción** (☎ 805-733-3713; admission $2; open 9am-5pm), trailhead for view-packed, 2-mile **El Camino Loop** trail into the mountains.

Beach bunnies will skip the mission, instead heading 14 scenic, winding miles west on Jalama Rd to **Jalama Beach** (☎ 805-736-8020; Jalama Rd; tent/RV sites $16/22, day-use $5), a gorgeous, sandy cove with scary-good surfing and RV-friendly campsites in the middle of nowhere. Heaven. There's even a convenience store.

Or, hold out for prettier (but less isolated) **Gaviota State Park** (☎ 805-899-1400; Hwy 1; tent sites $10, day-use $2) with unspectacular campsites, a spectacular beach (nudists should head south a bit) and even **sulfur warm springs**, via a short trail from the parking lot at the end of frontage road.

Hwy 1 joins Hwy 101 for the quick trip into Southern California proper, which is on fine display at **Refugio State Beach** and **El Capitan State Beach** (☎ 805-899-1400, reservations ☎ 800-444-7275; w www.reserve america.com; campsites $12), connected by a 2-mile hiking/biking trail.

Santa Barbara

POPULATION 90,000; MAP 7

An eternal beauty cradled by the Santa Ynez mountains, this Mediterranean-style village is the gateway to Southern California, defined here as the point at which surfers no longer need to wear wetsuits year-round. Downtown has outstanding architectural integrity, a masterpiece of a courthouse and noteworthy museums; the surrounding foothills offer great hiking and camping. When you see the view of the Channel Islands offshore, you'll agree – this may well be paradise.

SIGHTS

MISSION SANTA BARBARA
This isn't just another mission – this is *the* mission, with the most beautiful view (red-tiled roofs and lush trees set against the sparkling Pacific), the loveliest architecture and most impressive artwork.

☎ 805-682-4713; 2201 Laguna St; donations appreciated; open 9am-5pm

SANTA BARBARA MUSEUM OF ART
Among the finest (if not largest) art museums in the country, this two-century-old adobe structure houses works by Matisse, Chagall, Hopper and O'Keeffe.

☎ 805-963-4364; 1130 State St; adult/child $7/3; open 11am-5pm Tue-Sun

CHUMASH CAVES
Difficult to reach but worth the effort, these murals may have tracked the stars, or may have been part of an experimental Chumash artist's trippy decor.

Take Hwy 154 north to Painted Cave Rd, then follow it 12 winding miles to a tiny, hand-painted sign hung overhead reading 'cave.'

BEACHES
It seems there's no end to sea and sand in Santa Barbara – and that's just **West Beach**, west of the wharf and broad enough for a whole range of bums. At **Loon Point Beach**, 6 miles south in Summerland, wear your swimsuit or birthday suit.

ACTIVITIES

RED TILE WALKING TOUR
It's true – there's a city ordinance requiring all roofs to resemble Taco Bell. It's pretty, though. Anyway, pick up a free Red Tile Tour map at the **Tourist Information Center** (☎ *805-965-3021;* |W| *www.sbchamber.org; 1 Garden St)* to explore some of the original adobes, many dating from the 1780s.

HIKING
Serious hikers and bikers should invest in a guide. There are scores of trails and they're gorgeous. A nice one is **Inspiration Point**, just above the mission: Take Mission Canyon Rd east and make a left on Tunnel Rd, where sandstone, hanggliders and gorgeous views await.

Nearby, 5-mile **Rattlesnake Canyon** follows cool, green Rattlesnake Creek to views of the Channel Islands. From Mission Canyon Rd, make a right on Los Conoas Rd to the trailhead at Skofield Park.

WHEEL FUN RENTALS
Rent mountain bikes ($8/hr, $18/five hrs), in-line skates ($7/12), boogie boards ($5/15) and lots of other fun stuff.

☎ 805-963-3700; 22 State St

SLEEPING

Passport Reservation Services *(800-793-7666)* can help you find a room.

SANTA BARBARA SUNRISE RV PARK
You'll pitch a tent in a parking lot, but it's close to downtown and the beach.

☎ 805-966-9954; 516 S Salinas St; campsites $38

HALEY COTTAGES
This new guesthouse is still getting its act together, but is acceptably clean and friendly – a great budget choice.

☎ 805-463-3586; 227 E Haley St; dorm beds $20, private rooms $40

HOTEL STATE STREET
It's pretty basic and you'll share a bathroom, but you can't beat the location.

☎ 805-966-0586; 121 State St; rooms $45-80

SAN ROQUE MOTEL
One of several budget hotels on upper State St, San Roque Motel is a great deal if beachfront accommodations just aren't worth the extra cash.

☎ 805-687-6611, 800-587-5667; 3344 State St; rooms $55-85

EL ENCANTO HOTEL & GARDEN VILLAS
This mountaintop retreat has luxurious cottages, koi ponds, enchanting gardens, great views – the works. Bonus: Famous people stay here.

☎ 805-687-5000, 800-346-7039; 1900 Lausen; cottages $350-1800

EATING

With more than 400 restaurants competing for your dollar, you're practically guaranteed good food.

FARMER'S MARKET
Enjoy fresh fruits and veggies on Saturday (cnr Santa Barbara & E Cota Sts, 8:30am-12:30pm) and Tuesday (cnr 5th Ave & State St; 4-7:30pm), too.

☎ 805-962-5354

NATURAL CAFE
It's got a chill vibe and vegetarian versions of traditionally meaty Mexican and Italian standards, plus delicious incarnations of brown rice.

☎ 805-962-9494; 508 State St; organic grub $4-7; open 11am-9:30pm

LA TOLTECA TORTILLA CHIP FACTORY
The best thing about having a car here is being able to get great tamales and tacos stuffed with exotic cuts of meat (like brain, for example), where the no-frills environment means all the money's going to make good grub.

☎ 805-963-0847; 616 E Haley St; Mexicatessan fast food $2-8

JOE'S
Five stars for this fine spot, with checkered tablecloths and home cooking – think prime rib, beef dip sandwiches and mashed potatoes – in very large portions.

☎ 805-966-4638; 536 State St; entrees $7-22; open 11am-midnight Mon-Sat, 4-11pm Sun

---

DETOUR: SOLVANG

Perhaps the towns of Santa Ynez Valley seem *too* down-to-Earth. Where's the historic downtown? Where are the antiques? Where's the theme?

Ah, handmade fudge lovers, do not despair: From Gaviota State Park, take Hwy 101 north to Buellton and jump on Hwy 246 east. Then just look for the windmills – I kid you not – on the horizon.

Solvang (population 5000), aka 'Little Denmark,' was found-ed in 1911 by authentic Danes, although the lace-trimmed sea of knickknack-packed Victorian overkill didn't come until later. Folks who insist on calling themselves 'travelers' instead of 'tourists' should stay well away.

But Solvang has culture! The Elverhöj Museum (☎ *805-686-1211; 1624 Elverhoy Way; admission free; open Wed-Sun 1-4pm*) has displays on Danes in America. It has B&Bs! Reserve yours through the Chamber of Commerce (☎ *800-468-6765;* **w** *www .solvangusa.com*). Heck, it's even got a mediocre mission.

Best of all, Solvang has Danish pastries: Arne's Famous Aebleskivers (☎ *805-688-4645; 1672 Copenhagen Dr; sweets $1-5; open 6am-5pm*) does grand aebleskivers (pastries served with jam), as well as strudles and kringles galore.

In fact, why don't you pick up some aebleskivers (or hand-made fudge) for your 'traveler' friends who insisted on spend-ing the day exploring real, gritty Lompoc. They'll need them.

SAGE & ONION

You'll have no problem finding good gourmet grub in this town, but this place is both healthy and tasty, with lots of veggie options for upscale Buddhists, a bit of Middle Eastern flair, plus local fish, wine and more.

☎ 805-963-1012; 34 E Ortega St; entrees $24-32; open 5:30-10pm

ENTERTAINMENT

There's a crawlable collection of clubs and pubs around lower State and Ortega Sts. Pick up a copy of the free *Santa Barbara Independent* (W www.independent.com) for zillions more listings.

RUBY'S CAFE

It's a great place to dance all night to live Latin music – acts come from as far as South America to play this class act.

☎ 805-962-9688; 734 State St

SOHO

This is another great place to see a more eclectic assortment of musicians, many of them local. Check their schedule online.

☎ 805-962-7776; W www.sohosb.com; 1221 State St

THE BREWHOUSE

Skip the more popular pubs with their khaki-clad patrons – off the beaten track is this recommended, downscale joint with excellent beer, budget gourmet cuisine and live music Wednesday through Sunday.

☎ 805-884-4664; 229 W Montecito St; entrees $6-16; open 11am-midnight

On the Road

The official stretch of **Rincon Beach County Park** *(Bates Rd)* is just OK, but provides unofficial access to Rincon Point, a top surf spot, and a popular nude beach just north. **Emma Wood State Beach** *(☎ 805-648-4807, reservations 800-444-7275;* W *www.reserveamerica.com; campsites $12)* features a string of breezy roadside campsites.

Ventura (population 103,000) has all the ingredients of a great beach town: a lively and well-preserved historic city center; the high-quality **Albinger Archaeological Museum** *(☎ 805-648-5823; 211 E Main St; open 10am-4pm Wed-Sun);* and entertaining **San Buenaventura State Beach**, a wide slice of heaven complete with a pier. There's even a mission, **San Buenaventura** *(☎ 805-643-4318; 211 E Main St; donations appreciated; open 10am-5pm).*

At press time, however, Ventura was a tad, well, sleazy. When I asked why clean, pleasant **Pacific Inn** *(☎ 805-653-0877; 350 Thompson Blvd; singles/doubles $98/128 summer, $58/68 winter)* was special, the owner answered, 'We don't rent by the hour.' I laughed, only later discovering that my slightly cheaper hotel actually did.

Developers have sterilized **Ventura Harbor Village**, 5 miles south of downtown, a prefabricated place with souvenirs, charters and **Boatel Bunk & Breakfast** *(☎ 805-630-2628; Ventura Harbor; boats $88-100),* where you can sleep on an antique watercraft.

It's also home to **Channel Islands National Park Headquarters** *(☎ 805-658-5730; 1901 Spinnaker; admission free; open 8:30am-5pm),* with creative displays about tidepools and pinnepeds, plus a 95-percent complete pygmy mammoth skeleton found on Santa Rosa Island. The observation deck is truly awesome.

Hwy 1 leaves Hwy 101 only to plow right into the stuccoed strip malls and megastores of **Oxnard** (population 160,000), until recently a fecund agricultural region. 'Thanks, Oxnard, for destroying my farm,' reads one hand-lettered sign. The historic downtown, one block off Hwy 1 along A St, between 3rd and 6th Sts, is worth a look.

Then, suddenly, the splendid coastline of the Santa Monica Mountains reveals itself. **Point Mugu State Park** (☎ 310-457-1324, 800-444-7275; W www.reserveamerica.com; 900 W PCH; day-use $2) has two excellent campsites, sunny **Thornhill Broom Beach** (campsites $7), popular with RVers, and **Sycamore Cove Beach** (campsites $12), farther from the beach but better for tents.

Ask at the information center for a free trail map, or try 7-mile **La Jolla Valley Loop**, with waterfalls and Indian caves, beginning across from Thornhill Broom Beach, or the kid-friendly, 2-mile **Scenic Trail** in Sycamore Canyon.

A local institution, **Neptune's Net** (☎ 310-457-3095; 42505 Pacific Coast Hwy; fast seafood $3-10; open 10am-8pm) serves big baskets of fried seafood with cold beer and great views.

You'll then enter **Leo Carillo State Beach** (☎ 818-880-0350, 800-444-7275; W www.reserveamerica.com; campsites $12, day-use $3), one of the prettiest campsites on the coast and trailhead for 6-mile, beachside **Nicholas Flat Trail**.

At the edge of the wilderness, and marked by an obscene mansion farm, begins 27-mile-long, mostly gorgeous, celebrity-filled **Malibu** (population 20,000). According to folks who know, the top celebrity-sighting spots (and this goes for all of LA County) include **supermarkets** (the Malibu Ralph's is a good one), **convenience stores** and **gas stations**.

You can go upscale or downscale in Malibu. If you've got money to burn, crash with the waves at swanky **Malibu Beach Inn** (☎ 310-456-6444; 22878 Pacific Coast Hwy; rooms start at $320), then make reservations at fabulous **Beaurivage** (☎ 310-456-5733; 26025 Pacific Coast Hwy; Mediterranean-fusion cuisine $14-32; open 5-11pm); Monday is opera night.

Or, save a bundle at **Malibu Beach RV Park** (☎ 310-456-6052; W www.maliburv.com; 25801 Pacific Coast Hwy; tent sites $20-25, RV sites $29-47), with spectacular views. Next door, **Malibu Market** (☎ 310-456-3430; 25653 Pacific Coast Hwy; fresh fish $3-8; open 11am-9pm) serves the best seafood in town, much of it deep fried.

There are also dozens of beautiful beaches, of which **Zuma Beach** (day-use $3) is the unabashed star. Other faves include **Point Dume** (day-use $3), with a very large rock and full frontal nudity; and riff-raff free **Paradise Cove** (day-use $20).

Malibu Creek State Park is a hiker's paradise; don't skip 5-mile **Rock Pool Loop** at Malibu Canyon State Park, which takes you to the site where M*A*S*H was filmed. **Topanga State Park** (day-use $5), at Malibu's southern border, about 5 miles north of Hwy 1 on Topanga Canyon Blvd, has another 40 miles of hiking trails. Grab a map at the entrance.

On the Road: Entering LA

The smog is thickening, the traffic is slowing and – oh, look! Isn't that Pamela Anderson? Maybe, maybe not, but one thing's for sure: You've made it to Los Angeles cruising a glittering stretch of Hwy 1 that's had more screen time than Kevin Bacon. I hope you're in a convertible.

This book covers primarily the beachfront property of the infamous metropolis; if you want to mainline the LA experience, see 'Detour: Into the Belly of the Beast' (p51). Long-term visitors will want to pick up a copy of Lonely Planet's *Los Angeles* city guide or *Los Angeles Condensed*. Also check out the *LA Weekly* ([w] www.laweekly.com), or any of the other free weeklies, for restaurant and events listings.

Santa Monica & Venice Beach

POPULATION 124,000; MAP 8

You've seen Santa Monica on television and the silver screen, a backdrop for bombshells and setting for sitcoms, where the bad guys get shot and the good guys get lucky. It's posh: Gentrification has replaced the 'People's Republic of Santa Monica' with upscale shopping. But it's still a great town.

Besides, bohemian fun can still be had just south, in colorful Venice Beach, where wisdom can be had for a song and a song can be had for a dollar, with tarot card readings just $9 more.

SIGHTS & ACTIVITIES

SANTA MONICA PIER

It's a landmark, it's a theme park, it's the symbol of Santa Monica. With quirky restaurants, bars and the world's first solar-powered roller coaster (plus lots of other rides), it's quite possibly the best first date in LA County.

☎ 310-260-8744; rides $2-4 each; open 10am-10pm Sun-Thu, 10am-midnight Fri-Sat

VENICE BOARDWALK

This oceanfront carnival is the single best argument against Prozac, displaying as it does humanity's rich inheritance of insanity: chainsaw jugglers, air-brush artists, the roller-skating, guitar-playing turban guy (hint: he'll leave you alone for a tip), singing fortune tellers, limbless breakdancers – oh, and there's a beach.

VENICE CANALS

This 16-mile network of canals, just south of S Venice Blvd, two blocks from the beach, was opened in 1905, complete with Italian gondolas. Today they still make for a gorgeous walk.

BERGAMOT STATION

Housed in an 1875 train station, this collection of cool art galleries – more than 40 at last count – hosts openings, parties, workshops and more. It's a perfect indoor stroll, especially if you hit the onsite **Santa Monica Museum of Art** (☎ *310-586-6488; www.smmoa.org; adult/child $4/2)*, which has some quirky curators.

☎ 310-453-7535; [w] www.bergamotstation.com; 2525 Michigan Ave; open 10am-6pm Tue-Sun

MUSEUM OF FLYING

This dangerously underfunded but remarkable museum features a fabulous collection of aircraft (and spacecraft, thanks to local movie producers), including a P-51 Mustang, a Stearman and more.

☎ 310-392-8822; 2772 Donald Douglas Loop N; adult/child $8/4 by donation; open 10am-5pm Sat-Sun, or by appointment

JOIN A STUDIO AUDIENCE
At the corner of Ocean Front Walk and 17th St, there's usually a stand giving away free tickets to watch the filming of shows like *Dr Phil*, *Girlfriends* and *Price Is Right*.

BLAZING SADDLES BIKE RENTALS
Right on the pier and ready to roll when you are, they've got free maps and rental bikes for $4 to $7 per hour.

☎ 310-393-9778; 320 Santa Monica Pier; open 9am-5pm

BOARDWALK SKATES
Need an excuse to stay in the sun? Rent skates ($5/12 hr/day), bikes ($5/15), surfboards ($5/15) or boogie boards ($5/12) right here.

☎ 310-450-6634; 201½ Ocean Front Walk; open 10am-6pm

SLEEPING

VENICE BEACH HOSTEL
It may not be the plushest hostel on Earth, but it's certainly in contention for 'best murals' award. Private rooms are huge, and some have kitchenettes.

☎ 310-452-3052; [W] www.venicebeachhostel.com; 1515 Pacific Ave; dorm beds $13, private rooms $34

HI-LOS ANGELES/SANTA MONICA HOSTEL
Clean, efficient and businesslike, this isn't exactly a relaxed hostelling experience. But they do organize lots of interesting group tours.

☎ 310-393-9913, 800-909-4776; [W] www.hiayh.org; 1436 2nd St; dorm beds $27/30 member/nonmember, private rooms $66/72

PACIFIC SANDS MOTEL
The closest thing to a budget motel in Santa Monica, this place is clean, pleasant and has nifty 1960s-style alcoves in every room.

☎ 310-395-6133; 1515 Ocean Ave; rooms start at $65/85 winter/summer

INN AT VENICE BEACH
It's one of the nicest spots around, with colorful rooms and balconies from which to watch the Venice Beach parade lurch by.

☎ 310-821-2557; [W] www.innatvenicebeach.com; 327 Washington Blvd; rooms start at $119/139 winter/summer

SHUTTERS ON THE BEACH
There are plenty of upscale accommodations in Santa Monica, but this one is right on the beach and home to modern art that gets the Getty jealous.

☎ 310-458-0030; [W] www.shuttersonthebeach.com; 1 Pico Blvd; rooms $380-3000

EATING

OUTBACK SHACK
Owned and operated by Sidney natives, this place serves cheap growlers (a sort of savory pastry) and expensive beer. There's also an $8 barbie on weekends.

☎ 310-396-6137; 909 Ocean Front Walk; growlers $5 open 10am-sunset

OMELETTE PARLOR
It's the best place in town for breakfast (expect a wait on weekends), with monstrously good omelets and hefty sandwiches, salads and burgers to boot.

☎ 310-399-7892; 2732 Main St; entrees $5-9; open 6am-3pm

JIMMY'S CAFE
This great new café does great breakfasts and budget gourmet sandwiches, plus – get this – tasty fat-free guacamole, made with peas.

☎ 310-917-3311; 1447 2nd St; entrees $6-9; open 7:30am-4pm

SCHATZI ON MAIN

The patio's lovely and the food is fine (go for the *Kaiserchnarrn* or *Zweibelrostbrate*), and you may even see owner Arnold Schwarzenegger practice his political shmooz.

☎ 310-399-4800; 3110 Main St; lunch $7-16, dinner $10-20; open 11am-9pm

ENTERTAINMENT

The best bars and clubs are due east of Santa Monica – real partiers will be up for the trip. But there's still plenty to do around town.

ART FLICKS

Santa Monica is in charge of screening all the foreign, art and independent flicks for the rest of LA:

NuArt (☎ *310-478-6379; 11272 Santa Monica Blvd):* The finest indies plus the Rocky Horror Picture Show at midnight Saturday

The Royal (☎ *310-394-8099; 11523 Santa Monica Blvd):* Artsy and/or European flicks

NuWilshire Cinema (☎ *310-394-8099; 1314 Wilshire Blvd):* Big foreign releases

Laemmle Theater (☎ *310-394-9741; 1332 2nd St):* Highbrow indie films

WILL GEER THEATRICUM BOTANICUM

Just northeast of Santa Monica and nestled in the sycamore trees, this outdoor amphitheater hosts a resident acting company composed of aspiring movie stars. If you'd prefer to see already established celebrities singing *Brigadoon*, check out what's on at the **Santa Monica Playhouse** (☎ *310-394-9779; 1211 4th St),* a more polished venue though, alas, indoors.

☎ 310-455-3723; 1419 N Topanga Canyon Blvd

TEMPLE BAR

Relax on a sofa at this Santa Monica spot and enjoy the local musicians nightly.

☎ 310-393-6611; 1026 Wilshire Blvd; cover $3-15

McCABE'S GUITAR SHOP

The shop is actually next-door; this intimate venue instead hosts the masters of the instrument, from Joni Mitchell to Johnny Lee Hooker. Unique.

☎ 310-828-4403; 3101 Pico Blvd; cover $10-25

HARVELLE'S

Since 1931, this hole-in-the-wall venue has hosted top-notch jazz, blues and R&B performers.

☎ 310-395-1676; 1432 4th St

On the Road

South of Santa Monica, Hwy 1 becomes Lincoln Boulevard and heads inland, past **Marina Del Rey** (population 11,000), where pleasure boaters dock to shop at the upscale Cape Cod–style strip mall, or stay at the luxury high-rise motels.

Next door is **Ballona Wetlands**, the city's last remaining marsh. Folks have been trying to develop it for years, but environmentalists refuse to give up the fight. And there are still great blue herons in LA.

Dockweiler State Beach has grand views of offshore drilling platforms from the RV-only campsite. Bonus: It's right beneath a prime LAX flight path, with jumbo jets cruising in so low that you can almost feel the breeze.

Hwy 1 then dips into the Sepulveda Tunnel, under one of the LAX runways; on the other side are airport hotels – and airport hotel bars – galore.

Make a left at Manhattan Beach Blvd for an upscale treat. **Manhattan Beach** (population 35,000) is the northern extent of the **South Bay**, which includes the communities of Hermosa and Redondo Beaches, all connected by the excellent **South Bay Bicycle Trail**.

Manhattan Blvd is lined with pricey shops and excellent bars, including the **Manhattan Beach Brewing Company** (☎ 310-798-2744; 124 Manhattan Beach Blvd; open 11:30-1am), known for its Beach Rat Red custom brew. The road then dips dizzyingly into an excellent stretch of sand with a pier perfect for checking out the hot volleyball action.

Accommodations are surprisingly reasonable: Try cramped but clean **Manhattan Beach Hotel** (☎ 310-545-9020; 4017 Highland Ave; rooms $65-115), just two blocks from the water, and have dinner at **Mama D's** (☎ 310-546-1494; 1125A Manhattan Ave; Italian entrees $8-15; open 11:30am-whenever Mon-Fri, 2pm-whenever Sat-Sun), with award-winning thin-crust pizza.

If it's all too highbrow for you, continue south to gritty and gorgeous **Hermosa Beach** (population 19,000), with tamer waves but a wilder scene. Grab a bunk at groovy **Surf City Hostel** (☎ 310-798-2323; 26 Pier Ave; dorm beds $17, private rooms $45), with great murals and an even better vibe, and get ready to party.

DETOUR: INTO THE BELLY OF THE BEAST

The beach communities just don't do LA justice; you must head east to see the city. Sunset Blvd is *the* classic cruise.

From Santa Monica, meander through green and affluent Brentwood to the I-405. Just north is LA's pride, the **Getty Center** (☎ 310-440-7300; ⓦ www.getty.edu; 1200 Getty Center Dr; admission free; open 10am-6pm Tue-Sun), or you can continue east through the stately mansions of Bel Air.

Westwood, home of **UCLA**, is worth exploring; make a right on Galey Ave, with great Persian restaurants, and loop back on Hilgard Ave to Sunset Blvd and Beverly Hills. Make a right on N Beverly Dr to explore opulent **Rodeo Drive**, or grab a Map to Stars' Homes from a street vendor for further adventures.

West Hollywood loves its **Sunset Strip**, where the billboards are as legendary as the bars. Carefully groomed grunge becomes actually grungy as you approach Hollywood.

Take a left on La Brea Ave, then right onto starry-sidewalked Hollywood Blvd, past famous **Mann's Chinese Theater**, then Little Russia, Little Armenia and Little Korea; Hollywood Blvd joins Sunset Blvd in the actual City of Los Angeles.

Cruise through the rapidly gentrifying neighborhood of **Silverlake** and into **Echo Park**, where the movie *Chinatown* took place. Just past Grand Ave, **Chinatown** is on your left.

East of the optimistically named LA River (it's entirely paved and usually dry) is **East LA**, the heart of Chicano Los Angeles: Sunset now fittingly goes by the name of Cesar E Chavez Blvd.

Dano's Beach Grill (☎ *310-937-5686; 1320 Hermosa Ave, Hermosa Beach; entrees $8-15; open 11:30am-11pm Tue-Thu, 11-1am Fri-Sun*) has live world music on weekends and great Polynesian food all the time, plus its own custom beer created by **Brewworks Lounge** (☎ *310-376-0406; 58 11th St; open 7-11pm Mon-Fri, 1-11pm Sat*), a pleasant yuppie hangout.

Headbangers head to the **Lighthouse Café** (☎ *310-372-6911; 30 Pier Ave*), the best place in the South Bay to catch live music. And that's just the beginning of your bar crawl – there are probably a dozen more watering holes within walking distance that are well worth exploring.

Redondo Beach (population 68,000) boasts a famous pier that's a bit more engaging than your average tourist trap, plus weird **Seaside Lagoon** (☎ *310-318-0681; 200 Portofino Way; adult/child $4/3*), heated by the nearby power plant.

South of Redondo Beach, Hwy 1 rolls inland, cutting off the beautiful **Palos Verdes Peninsula**. Consider cruising southwest along Palos Verdes Dr instead, along the constantly eroding waterfront.

Malaga Cove, just off Hwy 1, is a small wonder that seems almost pristine after the party beaches to the north. Architecture buffs will enjoy the **Wayfarer's Chapel** (☎ *310-377-1650; 5755 Palos Verdes Dr S*), designed by Lloyd Wright, Frank's son, overlooking **Abalone Cove**, where you can swim in the buff.

Continue along the coast to **San Pedro** (population 86,000), with a way-too-cutesy tourist quarter (the 'o' in **Ports O' Call Village** is your first clue) and the excellent **Los Angeles Maritime Museum** (☎ *310-548-7618; Berth 84; donations appreciated; open 10am-5pm Tue-Sun*), with some 700 models of famous ships.

San Pedro's most important site lies due east of the city, however: Exit Hwy 1 to I-110, then jump on Hwy 47 to Long Beach. This takes you over **Worldport LA** and the **Port of Long Beach**, together the third-largest port in the world. Big machines, big profits and big pollution: On a smoggy day, civilization's required toxicity will break your heart – or at least sting your eyes.

GHOST STORIES

Hundreds of ghosts agree: The California coast is *the* top spot to spend the afterlife. Here are some of the more famous hauntings along Hwy 1:

Moss Beach Distillery (*Moss Beach*): A lady in blue still floats through, looking for her lover.

Alcatraz (*San Francisco*): Torture and humiliate enough men, and the pain will long outlive them.

Two Harbors (*Catalina Island*): Actress Natalie Wood still puts on the occasional performance.

Roosevelt Hotel (*Hollywood*): The choice of celebrity spirits, Marilyn Monroe still does her makeup while Montgomery Clift bugles.

Queen Mary (*Long Beach*): Photos might capture a young workman crushed in Shaft Alley, or the white-clad beauty in the Queen's Salon.

Long Beach

POPULATION 450,000; MAP 1

At first glance, Long Beach seems a bit more businesslike than the other beaches. Tailored suits and sensible heels are a uniform marched from gleaming high-rise to gleaming high-rise – you're not in Venice anymore.

Then you notice that every restaurant on Pine St becomes a dance club after 10pm. And then, there's the sweet surreality of the *Queen Mary* anchored offshore. Yep, underneath the suits, it's still a beach town.

SIGHTS & ACTIVITIES

This is a fun town, but note that the beach, while long, isn't the nicest.

RMS *QUEEN MARY*

The finest floating tourist trap in California, this 1000-foot-long luxury hotel has regular tours, ghost tours (the boat is haunted, but the tour relies on special effects), fine dining and fabulous accommodations. Bonus: The Russian submarine *Scorpion* can also be toured for another $10.

☎ 310-435-3511; 1126 Queen's Hwy; tours $8/5 adult/child; rooms $99-129 without view, $159-650 with view; open 10am-6pm

AQUARIUM OF THE PACIFIC

This is one of the finest aquariums in the country, with tanks simulating 17 different undersea biomes populated by just about every fish you can think of. Better, you can add a behind-the-scenes tour or 90-minute boat ride to your visit.

☎ 562-590-3100; W www.aquariumofthepacific.org; 100 Aquarium Way; adult/child $19/10; open 9am-6pm

MUSEUM OF LATIN AMERICAN ART

With an impressive permanent collection and innovative temporary exhibitions that range from sculpture and printmaking to abstract installation pieces, this is a top venue for artists from Central and South America as well as the USA.

☎ 562-437-1689; W www.molaa.com; 628 Alamitos Ave; adult/child $5/3; open 11:30am-6pm

NAPLES

Just south of Long Beach, this posh suburb has canals – like Venice Beach, only without the homeless people. **Gondola Getaway** (☎ *562-433-9595;* W *www.gondolagetawayinc.com; 5437 Ocean Blvd; couple $65*) will pole you around.

SLEEPING & EATING

The most prestigious address in town is the *Queen Mary,* but there are many other upscale choices.

HI-LOS ANGELES/SOUTH BAY HOSTEL

It's worth the drive to stay in this clean, quiet San Pedro hostel jutting out into the Pacific; guests can use their mountain bikes.

☎ 310-831-8109; 3601 S Gaffey St No 613; dorm beds $15/18 member/non-member, private rooms $40

DOCKSIDE BOAT & BED

So the *Queen Mary* isn't good enough for you – you need your own personal watercraft. Let the waves rock you to sleep on this unusual B&B, which puts you up in a rustic sailboat for the night.

☎ 562-436-3111; W www.boatandbed.com; Rainbow Harbor, Dock 5, 316 E Shoreline Dr; boats $175-240

GEORGE'S GREEK DELI
Checkered tablecloths and great food are accompanied by Greek folk music on Thursday and belly dancing Saturday night.

☎ 562-437-1184; 318 Pine Ave; lunch $4-8, dinner $7-13; open 7am-11pm

WASABI JAPANESE RESTAURANT
If you can't get to the best sushi – and karaoke – in town, they'll send their hot rod limousine up to 5 miles and pick you up, free of charge. Please tip the driver.

☎ 562-901-0300; 200 Pine Ave; lunch $6-15, dinner $16-28; open 11:30am-11pm

On the Road

Soon after leaving Long Beach, you'll find yourself ensconced in California's Republican stronghold, derided by its northern neighbors as the endless suburb, the cultural wasteland, the eternal mall – the fashion faux-pas. Orange County gets no respect.

But behind the Orange Curtain lie treasures worth exploring, from the **Richard Nixon Presidential Library & Birthplace** (☎ 714-993-3393; 18001 Yorba Linda Blvd; adult/child $7/4; open 10am-5pm) to **Little Saigon** (cnr Hwy 22 & I-405), with the largest concentration of quality pho restaurants outside Vietnam. And did we mention those beaches?

Seal Beach (population 25,000), with a fine beach, pier and pleasant downtown, is worth a quick jaunt westward. Nature lovers can continue south to **Bolsa Chica Ecological Preserve**, with a lush 2-mile loop through the wetlands.

DETOUR: SANTA CATALINA ISLAND

When chewing gum gazillionaire William Wrigley Jr purchased this island in 1919 – building a casino and the port-resort of Avalon – he inadvertently preserved an irreplaceable eco-system. Today, more than two-thirds of this Channel Island remains undeveloped, and it's all just an hour from LA.

Catalina Express (☎ 310-519-1212, 800-464-4228; w www.catalinaexpress.com; roundtrip $45/34 adult/child) runs boats from San Pedro, Long Beach and Dana Point to Avalon, Catalina's biggest city, and less frequently to smaller Two Harbors, with spotty service in the off-season.

Avalon is a colorful confection of souvenir shops and somewhat overpriced restaurants and accommodations, with the exception of fine **Hermosa Hotel** (☎ 310-510-1010, 888-684-1313; 131 Metropole St; rooms $25-85 winter, $50-155 summer).

There are also five **campsites** (☎ 310-510-0303; w www.catalina.com\camping; campsites $10/16 low/high season) on the island; most require at least a 1-mile walk. The best are near **Two Harbors**, Catalina's second city, as are the island's finest hikes. This small town, with a few hotels and restaurants, is a good choice for visitors eager to avoid Avalon's crowds.

The mellow communities of **Surfside** and **Sunset** line the highway with sandy budget hotels, downscale diners, and kayak, surfboard and bicycle rental shops.

Huntington Beach

POPULATION 190,000; MAP 9

It's just another case of unbridled development threatening something special, a perfect beach town long known for its totally awesome surf and a totally relaxed vibe.

But the Main St strip has been stuccoed an unnerving pink and packed with chain restaurants, theoretically to suit the tastes of upwardly mobile professionals, who look for all the world like beach bums and bunnies stuffed uncomfortably into business suits.

SIGHTS & ACTIVITIES

HUNTINGTON PIER
It's the best vantage point for surfer-watching in Orange County, particularly during September's **Ocean Pacific Pro Surf** competition.

INTERNATIONAL SURFING MUSEUM
With a bitchin' collection of historic surfboards, surfwear and surf music, this tiny museum totally rules.

☎ 714-960-3483; 411 Olive Ave; adult/child $2/1; open noon-5pm

SURFING WALK OF FAME
It's like Hollywood Blvd, except you need skill and talent to get here. A statue of Duke Kahanamoku, the Hawaiian surf champion who brought the sport to Huntington, presides over the handprints of renowned waveriders.

HUNTINGTON SURF & SPORT
Inspired? Rent a surfboard ($6/20 hr/day). Don't know how? Splurge on some surf lessons through **Rockin' Fig Surf** (☎ 714-536-1048; 316 Main St).

☎ 714-841-4000; 300 Pacific Coast Hwy; open 8am-10pm

SLEEPING & EATING

More than a dozen budget hotels line Hwy 1, with rates reflecting how often sand is vacuumed from the creaky beds.

HUNTINGTON CITY BEACH
Dude – you can camp on the beach! Unprotected tent and RV sites are just steps away from those legendary waves.

☎ 714-536-5280; cnr 1st St & Hwy 1; campsites $16

COLONIAL INN HOSTEL
This hostel has a spare room for your boards! Free toast and no lockout make this the choice of, like, a whole bunch of world-class surfers.

☎ 714-536-3315; W www.huntingtonbeachhostel.com; 421 8th St; dorm beds $18-20

SUGAR SHACK
This Huntington Beach institution has been dishing up big breakfasts before the big breaks for years; their accumulation of artifacts is worth a look.

☎ 714-536-0355; 213 Main St; entrees $4-11; open 7am-3pm

PHO MY MAN
This place serves good, authentic Vietnamese soups and vegetarian dishes.

☎ 714-536-4370; 300 Pacific Coast Hwy; open 10am-10pm

Newport Beach

POPULATION 75,000; MAP 9

Just a few sun-drenched miles south of Huntington Pier, this is a show-case for affluent OC. Beautiful and bourgeois, the city surrounds Newport Bay, cradling islands that boast some of the most impressive property values on the planet.

There are two Newport Beaches, however: The first is based on exclusive Balboa Island, with all the shopping, dining and yachting necessary to keep up with the Joneses in Beverly Hills. But the other, built along Balboa Peninsula and Newport Pier, is totally ready to party when you are.

SIGHTS & ACTIVITIES

BALBOA ISLAND

The ultimate gated community (it's got a moat!) still welcomes even the scroungiest souls to its upscale shopping and dining area. That's OC for you – wealth without pretensions.

BEACHES

Protected **Balboa Beach**, on Balboa Island, is perfect for families, while **Newport Beach**, at Newport Pier, is lined with headshops and bars like **Matt Lynch's** (☎ 949-675-1556; 2300 W Oceanfront; pub grub $4-7; open 7am-midnight), serving schooners of beer. The most famous surf around is at **The Wedge**, at the end of Ocean Blvd, where waves reach 20 brutal feet.

BALBOA FUN ZONE

This wacky collection of vintage attractions, most built in 1936, really is fun. Kids like the Ferris wheel and bumper cars, while adults can charter whale-watching and fishing trips at the nearby docks.

cnr Bay Ave and Palm St

NEWPORT HARBOR NAUTICAL MUSEUM

All nautical museums should be in boats, and this sternwheeler houses some excellent (if low-budget) exhibits about all things maritime, from the history of the America's Cup to crab fishing in the Pacific. It's a labor of love, not the Smithsonian, and perhaps more enjoyable for the effort.

☎ 949-673-7863; 151 E Coast Hwy; adult/child $4/1; open 10am-5pm Tue-Sun

SLEEPING & EATING

NEWPORT DUNES RESORT

Roughing it? Hardly! Enjoy a private swimming lagoon, kayaking, bike rentals and a marketplace selling, among other things, prepared sushi, all right by your tent.

☎ 949-729-3863; W www.newportdunes.com; 1131 Back Bay Dr; tent sites $38-58, RV sites $55-90

LITTLE INN BY THE BAY

With pretty, frilly rooms featuring microwave and refrigerator, plus free mountain bikes for guests, this may be the best deal in town.

☎ 949-673-8800; W www.littleinnbythebay.com; 2627 Newport Blvd; rooms $69-129 Sun-Thu, $89-199 Fri-Sat

PORTOFINO HOTEL

This elegant splurge makes up for the coziness of its rooms with awesome views and very tasteful amenities. Best of all, just because you want a nice room doesn't mean you have to hang out on Balboa Island.

☎ 949-723-4370; 2306 Oceanfront Blvd; rooms start at $150/260 winter/summer

CHARLIE'S CHILI
The good greasy grub has kept vacationing families and stoned surfers return-ing for years. The 'all-u-can-eat' bowl of Ideal Chili ($5) makes Wednesday special.

☎ 949-675-7991; 2104 W Oceanfront Blvd; diner dishes $4-9; open 7am-midnight Sun-Thu, 7-3am Fri-Sat

WILMA'S PATIO
The best breakfast on Balboa Island boasts omelets, egg enchiladas and the Balboa Belly Bomber, which can sustain a high-fashion model for over a week.

☎ 949-675-5542; 225 Marine Ave; dazzling diner food $3-15; open 7am-9pm

CRAB COOKER
The very best way to eat the catch of the day is fried to perfection and served up hot and greasy on a paper plate. Lines may be long, but it's well worth the wait.

☎ 949-673-0100; 2200 Newport Blvd; seafood & fast food $6-22

On the Road

With Newport Beach behind you, you may wonder what all those mansions are doing in front of you. It's **Corona del Mar**, with truly fabulous beaches – complete with rock arches and volleyball tournaments – lining Ocean Blvd, and the exquisite botanicals of **Sherman Library & Gardens** (☎ 949-673-2261; 2647 E Pacific Coast Hwy; adult/child $4/1; open 10:30am-4pm).

Crystal Cove State Park (☎ 949-494-3539; walk-in tent sites $7, day-use $3) offers an underwater park popular with divers, and excellent hiking. Try the mellow, shady, 4-mile **Moro Canyon Loop** trail, great for kids.

Laguna Beach

POPULATION 24,000; MAP 9

Laguna has been an art colony since the early 1900s, when Norman St Claire's watercolors of the area's impressive coastline drew artists from all over the country. By 1918, there was an art association, and by 1933, a world-class art competition that's still the city's top draw.

SIGHTS & ACTIVITIES

LAGUNA ART MUSEUM
Yes, there are lots of landscapes at this excellent museum, but rotating exhibits include California car culture (very Orange County) and multi-artist perspectives on being white in America.

☎ 949-494-8971; W www.lagunaartmuseum.org; 307 Cliff Dr; adult/child $7/5; open 11am-5pm

ART GALLERIES
More than 50 art galleries are concentrated along Ocean St east of Hwy 1. Pick up a gallery guide anywhere, or join the monthly **Gallery Walk** (☎ 949-497-0716; W www.firstthursdayartwalk.com; 6-9pm), on the first Thursday of the month.

BEACHES
With some 30 public beaches strung along Hwy 1, it's hard to choose. Favorites include **Victoria Beach**, home to the 1926 La Tour tower; **Main Beach**, with snack stands and lifeguards; and **Diver's Cove**, beneath the bluff at beautifully landscaped Heisler Park, and known for its undersea scenery.

BREWERIES
Artists need lots of inspiration, which is why Laguna has two great brewpubs: **Laguna Beach Brewing Company** (☎ 949-499-2337; 422 S Coast Hwy; pub

grub $5-15; open 11:30am-11:30pm Sun-Thu, 11:30am-2am Fri-Sat) has magic shows on Saturday night, while **Ocean Brewing Company** *(☎ 949-497-3381; 237 Ocean Ave; Italian cuisine $6-20)* has live music almost nightly.

SLEEPING & EATING

HOTEL LAGUNA
It's right on the beach, it's got a spa, and they actually deliver your continental breakfast to your room.

☎ 949-494-1151; W www.hotellaguna.com; 425 S Coast Hwy; rooms $110-200 summer, $80-165 other times

EILER'S INN
This honeymoon-worthy B&B does it right: unusual antiques, excellent breakfasts and gorgeous gardens with a perfect view.

☎ 949-494-3004; W www.eilersinn.com; 741 S Coast Hwy; rooms $130-260 summer, $95-175 other times

LAS BRISAS
Next to the Laguna Art Museum, this local favorite has one of the best views on the coast. Enjoy Mexican seafood, soft tacos or, best of all, the awesome breakfast buffet.

☎ 949-497-5434; 361 Cliff Dr; dinner $15-28, other meals $7-15; open 9am-3pm & 5-10pm

COTTAGE RESTAURANT
Laguna definitely knows how to do breakfast – try the cranberry-orange pancakes for a treat. Other entrees are down-to-Earth gourmet.

☎ 949-494-3023; 308 N Coast Hwy; dinner $10-22, other meals $5-10; open 11:30am-9pm

End of the Road: Dana Point

POPULATION 36,000; MAP 9

The end of the road (or the beginning, depending on your orientation), is an inauspicious finale, dividing into tracts of typically Orange County–style economansions. But there are a few pleasant ways to say farewell to the prettiest ribbon of concrete in the state of California.

GOT ART?

Laguna's landmark event is the **Festival of the Arts** *(☎ 949-497-6582, 800-487-3378; W www.foapom.com; $7/5; open 10am-11:30pm Jul-Aug)*, a seven-week juried exhibit of 160 top artists.

The strangest and most popular attraction is the **Pageant of Masters**, where human models are blended seamlessly into re-creations of famous paintings. Order tickets ($10-60) early.

In the 1960s, local artists who couldn't quite make the cut decided to have their own exhibition right across the street, the **Sawdust Art Festival** *(☎ 949-494-3030; W www.sawdustartfestival.org; 935 Laguna Canyon Rd; $7/2; open 10am-10pm Jul-Aug)*. Lower prices and fewer pretensions actually draw larger crowds.

A third art festival, the **Art-A-Fair Festival** *(☎ 949-494-4514; W www.art-a-fair.com; 777 Laguna Canyon Rd; $5/4; open 10am-9pm Jul-Aug)*, focuses on watercolors, pastels and oil paintings.

SIGHTS & ACTIVITIES

MISSION SAN JUAN CAPISTRANO
Among the loveliest in Father Serra's chain, this recently renovated mission has an excellent museum and parade every March 19 to celebrate the swallows' return. Sadly, construction led the birds to relocate to San Fernando Valley.

☎ 949-248-2048; 31882 Camino Capistrano; $6/4; open 8:30am-4pm

BEACHES
Three white-sand beaches stretch along the last of Hwy 1: **Salt Creek County Beach**, near the Ritz-Carlton, is perfect for a picnic; **Doheny State Beach** has sweet campsites; and **Capistrano Beach** has the cheapest parking.

SLEEPING & EATING

DOHENY STATE BEACH
Just off the freeway is one of the finer oceanfront campsites in Southern California – make reservations well in advance.

☎ 949-496-6171, 800-444-7275; W www.reserveamerica.com; campsites $19

THE RITZ-CARLTON LAGUNA NIGUEL
Even the Ritz didn't want to admit it was in Dana Point, but here it is, with grand views of the Pacific and suites that include amenities like grand pianos. There are also several gourmet restaurants onsite.

☎ 949-240-2000, 800-241-3333; 1 Ritz-Carlton Dr; rooms start at $370

OLAMENDI'S
This famed taqueria, across from Capistrano Beach, may actually top the Ritz's cuisine.

☎ 949-661-1005; 34660 Pacific Coast Hwy; Mexican fast food $3-9; open 11am-8pm

AURORA'S TAQUERIA
This taqueria on the northbound side of Hwy 1 does great carne asada and potato quesadillas, but the specialty is menudo, served weekends only.

☎ 949-496-1401; 34146 Pacific Coast Hwy; Mexican fast food $2-5; open 7am-8pm

On the Road

Just because Hwy 1 ends doesn't mean *you* have to stop. Though I-5 isn't exactly charming, it's your best connection to California's coast.

Can't-miss sites farther south include Oceanside's **California Surf Museum**, the mellow beach town of **Leucadia** and, in Del Mar, the geological wonder of **Torrey Pines State Beach**. Walk south to **Black's Beach**, San Diego's favorite spot for an all-over tan.

San Diego has attractions aplenty, including ritzy **La Jolla Cove**; **Balboa Park**, with a grand collection of museums occupying the site of the 1915 Panama-California Exposition; the world famous **San Diego Zoo** and **Wild Animal Park**; and the haunted **Hotel del Coronado**.

Mission Beach, with its famous wooden roller coaster, and **Ocean Beach**, where Sunset Cliffs provide the best ending possible to any day, are just a few fine communities along the coast. By now, you're only 20 minutes from **Tijuana**, Mexico, where you can continue south along the M-1.

Think about your priorities: Is there anything you really need to get done in the next couple of months? You only live once. And **Cabo San Lucas** has some very nice beaches....

The Author

Paige R Penland is a freelance writer who has lived in San Diego, Los Angeles and Oakland, California, and considers herself something of a coastline connoisseur. Between ill-advised tanning sessions and embarrassing boogie-board incidents, she's also managed to write a handful of travel guides for Lonely Planet Publications, as well as the monthly 'Wander Woman' travel column for chickclick.com and *Lowrider* magazine's *History of Lowriding*.

From the Author:

First, I'd like to thank Mariah Bear and Kathleen Munnelly for the opportunity to research and write about some of California's best beaches. Thanks also to Michelle and Ashlea Gaspard for their hospitality, and Patrick Huerta for all his help with the maps.

The Lonely Planet Story

The story begins with a classic travel adventure: Tony and Maureen Wheeler's 1972 journey across Europe and Asia to Australia. There was no useful information about the overland trail then, so Tony and Maureen published the first Lonely Planet guidebook to meet a growing need.

From a kitchen table, Lonely Planet has grown to become the largest independent travel publisher in the world, with offices in Melbourne (Australia), Oakland (USA), London (UK) and Paris (France).

Today Lonely Planet guidebooks cover the globe. There is an ever-growing list of books and information in a variety of media. Some things haven't changed. The main aim is still to make it possible for adventurous travelers to get out there – to explore and better understand the world.

At Lonely Planet we believe travelers can make a positive contribution to the countries they visit – if they respect their host communities and spend their money wisely. Since 1986 a percentage of the income from each book has been donated to aid projects and human rights campaigns, and, more recently, to wildlife conservation.

www.lonelyplanet.com

Lonely Planet's award-winning Web site has information on hundreds of destinations from Amsterdam to Zimbabwe, complete with interactive maps and color photographs. You'll also find the latest travel news, an online shop with all our titles, and a lively bulletin board where you can meet fellow travelers, swap recommendations and seek advice.

About This Book

Commissioned and developed by Kathleen Munnelly • Edited by Rachel Bernstein • Design and layout by Candice Jacobus & Wendy Yanagihara • Maps by Annette Olson & Bart Wright • Cover design by Candice Jacobus • Series Publishing Manager: Maria Donohoe • Thanks to Ruth Askevold, Mariah Bear, Andreas Schueller, Ryan ver Berkmoes and Vivek Waglé

LONELY PLANET

You already know that Lonely Planet produces more than this one guidebook, but you might not be aware of the other products we have on this region. Here is a selection of titles that you may want to check out as well:

California
ISBN 1-86450-331-9
US$21.99 · UK£13.99

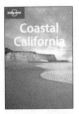

Coastal California
Available Jan 2004
ISBN 1-74059-468-1
US$18.99 · UK£11.99

San Francisco
ISBN 1-74104-154-6
US$17.99 · UK£11.99

Los Angeles
ISBN 1-74059-021-X
US$15.99 · US£9.99

HIT THE ROAD WITH LONELY PLANET'S OTHER ROAD TRIP TITLES:

Road Trip: Route 66
ISBN 1-74059-580-7
US$10.00 · UK£5.99

Road Trip: Napa & Sonoma Wine Country
ISBN 1-74059-581-5
US$10.00 · UK£5.99

INDEX